And Now a Few Laughs from Our Sponsor

And Now a Few Laughs from Our Sponsor

The Best of Fifty Years of Radio Commercials

Larry Oakner

John Wiley & Sons, Inc.

Published by John Wiley & Sons, Inc., New York.
Published simultaneously in Canada.

Library of Congress Cataloging-in-Publication Data:
Oakner, Larry.
  And now a few laughs from our sponsor / Larry Oakner.
    p. cm.
  "An Adweek book."
  Includes bibliographical references and index.
  ISBN 0–471-20218-5 (cloth : alk. paper)
  1. Broadcast advertising.   2. Humor in advertising.   I. Title.

HF6146.B74 O16 2002
659.14'2'0973—dc21   2002024979

Printed in the United States of America.

10 9 8 7 6 5 4 3 2 1

And Now a Few Laughs from Our Sponsor

In memory of my mother and father,
Mervyn and Helaine Oakner, my original producers

In loving thanks to my family—
Barbara, Saara, and Jesse—for staying tuned in

Contents

Preface: When I First Tuned In — ix

Acknowledgments — xvii

Introduction: Laughter Is Good for Business — xix

① When Advertising First Got Funny — 1

② Piels Beer: The Fresh and Timely Humor of Bob and Ray — 9

③ Contadina Tomato Paste: Stan Freberg Takes Comedy Seriously — 27

④ Bell Brand Potato Chips: Mal Sharpe's Interviews Are Fresh, Crisp, and Yummy — 41

⑤ Blue Nun Wine: Stiller and Meara Give a Product a Personality — 61

⑥ *Time* Magazine: Dick and Bert Showcase Fanatical Devotion — 73

⑦ Laughing Cow Cheese: Joy Golden Writes the Way People Really Talk — 97

⑧ Molson Beer: Anne Winn and Garrett Brown Understand Good Timing — 115

⑨ Motel 6: The Richards Group Leaves a Light On for the Brand — 135

⑩   Ortho Antstop Fire Ant Killer: Radio Savant Goes
        Straight for the Announcer   153
⑪   Have You Heard the Latest?: The Fundamentals
        of Radio's Future   167

        Bibliography   199
        Contacts   201
        CD Tracks and Credits   205
        Index   207
        About the CD-ROM   213
        About the Author   215

Preface: When I First Tuned In

I have radio in my genes.

My father, Mervyn Oakner, began his career as a radio broadcasting journalist at the microphone of the *Denver Post*'s first radio news venture in the late 1940s. As he moved from journalism to public relations to advertising, he used his experience to bring innovative uses of radio to clients of his Los Angeles advertising agency, Anderson-McConnell-Oakner in the 1960s. I never thought it was unusual growing up reading copies of *Advertising Age* and the Los Angeles ad trade pub, *MAC*. My dad would regularly bring home radio scripts and a clunky, portable Wollensack reel-to-reel tape recorder to review commercials for his clients, such as the California Avocado Growers ("Calavo Avocado Guacamole . . . Dip!), the Southern California Rambler dealers (tying in with a story record about a maniacal Nash Rambler that went "beep-beep"), and the jingle he wrote for the Southern California grocery chain, Thriftimart ("Every day's a special day at Thriftimart . . ."). Once he even brought home a promotional record album created in the early sixties by the CBS radio network that desperately pitched ad agencies on the viability and efficiency of radio advertising, as sponsors abandoned the medium for the visual power of television. The album, titled *Let's Run It Up the Flag-*

pole and See Who Salutes, was written in large part by copy-writer/lyricist Alan Alch as a send-up of a Broadway show about an advertising agency where the janitor, Gugglielmo Marconi, accidentally breaks the picture tube on a TV set and inadvertently "invents" the previously unknown medium of radio. The long-lost record piqued my interest even as a kid and has stuck in my head to this day.

When I went off to college in the seventies, I had my own opportunity to participate in the magic of radio and the burgeoning world of FM broadcasting. At the Santa Barbara campus of the University of California, I volunteered to be the morning newscaster for the low-watt FM station, KCSB-FM. Ripping and reading the headlines at 7:30 A.M. to a bunch of hungover students was as much an exercise in counterculture media as it was an FCC-required responsibility for the station to broadcast any news, especially when we found stories about drug busts and antigovernment rallies. But what I truly enjoyed was creating the promotions and commercials for campus activities, as well as having the chance to write and produce with a partner an entire original radio play. The script was a loose amalgam of bad jokes, corny sound effects, and trippy skits that was so close to what my idols at the Firesign Theater were doing that it should have been called plagiarism. When I moved back to Los Angeles, I was still enthralled by the spoken word on radio, tuning in whenever I could to listen to Peter Bergman and Phil Austin of the Firesign Theater reading from Carlos Castaneda's early peyote-inspired works on the Los Angeles station KPFK, the alternative Pacifica radio station.

After college, I followed in my father's path and began a career in advertising. I worked as a junior copywriter at Benton & Bowles in Los Angeles, where I got my first chance to create radio commercials for Continental Airlines; I even did remote recordings, directing Dodger great Don Drysdale and announcer Dick Enberg at the ballpark reading *my* radio copy for the Proud Bird with the Golden Tail, Continental Airlines. Boy, did I have a lot to learn!

And learn I did, by listening to the people whom I admired most. People like Dick Orkin and Bert Berdis, who were taking the ad world by storm in the mid-to-late seventies with their silly story–based radio commercials for *Time* magazine and other clients. I still have the original Eva-Tone sound sheets—a kind of floppy vinyl magazine insert that could be played like a record— that Dick and Bert did as a bartered promotion for their fledgling company. I cut my teeth on Stan Freberg, whose reputation for innovation and creativity was already legendary by the time I was old enough to learn from his commercial spoofs and real spots. I was also fortunate enough to work for talented people such as Bob Klein of *Klein &*, who taught me how to direct radio voice talent with graciousness, humor, and charm, and Tania Presby, my first impressively theatrical creative director, who taught me how to let go of pretentious "radio" writing and find my own natural style. Along the way, I studied the scripts of award-winning commercials included in many a *Communication Arts* annual.

In my own career, I sometimes had the chance to trade on my father's professional connections, working with some of the same radio people he did. For the Oregon electric utility, Pacific Power and Light, I created a series of spots with the inimitable Mal Sharpe, whose man-on-the-street ambush humor was perfect for a campaign that asked bewildered Oregonians what electricity tasted and smelled like. I got the chance to hire and work with the great voice and radio talent Alan Barzman. I also found my own radio geniuses, like the Seattle-based composer and avant-garde sound designer, Norm Durkee, who worked with me on a bizarre ad-libbed campaign for The Antique Boutique, a New York vintage clothing company, that featured the voices of his nonprofessional friends acting out their clothing dreams, memories, and fantasies to Durkee's original musical compositions.

Over the course of my professional experience, I have written, directed, and produced hundreds of radio commercials. Although I had a few successes at comedy, I found my style was better suited to narrative commercials. Along the way, I won a number of local, regional, and national awards, including a Finalist honor at the Radio-Mercury Awards for some commercials I created for the Chubb Group of Insurance Companies that linked personal property insurance with opera and symphonic music and aired on a classical music station. I wrote spots that used the mechanical engine sounds of Caterpillar earthmoving equipment to play a Christmas carol. I cast a Jewish "Molly Goldberg" voice-over actress to sell Honeybaked Hams®. And I shilled for more political causes than I'd care to remember. I was lucky enough to work with famous voice-over actors, as well as some who truly needed speech therapy. And I watched technology change from sticking bits of quarter-inch tape together to digital recording to Internet media placement. Through it all, I always enjoyed creating something out of the words, the music, the sound effects, and the voices—creating emotion, sales, and persuasion out of thin air.

All of my experience, passion, historical knowledge, and joy of radio advertising came together when I was hired as an adjunct instructor to teach radio copywriting at the Fashion Institute of Technology at State University of New York in Manhattan. I began the first class of each semester the same way—by asking the undergrads if they listened to radio. All the hands would go up. Then I'd ask who would change the radio station when a commercial started to air. All the hands would go up again. I'd tell them that their goal by the end of the semester was to learn how to make commercials good enough so that they wouldn't change the station.

Although there are a couple of textbooks on the subject of radio copywriting, they offer only a bit of radio history, the basics of format, and some exercises on scripting. Even though they do include some examples of commercials, what the works lack is a sense of historical context for the commercials. It is impossible to create good radio commercials—particularly the kind of humorous radio that everyone wants to create—without understanding their historical precedents. Even recently published popular and detailed histories of radio devote scant coverage to radio advertising over the past 50 years. To fill in the gaps, I would bring into my classes some of my collection of CDs and tapes of radio commercials by masters like Freberg, Dick and Bert, Bob and Ray, and others from the fifties, sixties, seventies, and eighties. Not only had the students never heard of these creative geniuses, but they didn't understand the humor or have a familiarity with the context. Radio is an ephemeral and temporal medium, and what was hot topical humor in Bob and Ray's spots for Piels beer in 1959 is lost on someone whose sense of history extends only to what happened over the past two years. I knew that the history of comedy radio advertising needed chronicling.

I couldn't bear the thought of radio advertising's humorous history disappearing. That was the inspiration for this book and the free CD accompanying it: I wanted to include a historical perspective of the commercials, insights into the creative process that produced the spots, a look at the creative geniuses who created them, and the lessons they could impart to young copywriters. I wanted to put the jokes into context and help people understand why the commercials were successful then and memorable today. I want to share my love, passion, and interest in preserving one of the great traditions of radio advertising with students of radio copywriting, with my advertising and broadcasting colleagues, with aficionados of radio history, and with anyone who has ever chuckled or grinned while listening to a radio commercial.

The process of writing this historical chronicle naturally included long hours scanning old newspaper and magazine articles about the featured, yet nearly forgotten commercials. When I could find them, I was fortunate enough to interview the people who were responsible for writing, acting, and producing the commercials themselves. They graciously offered their help in locating other people involved in making their commercials, from musicians to clients to sound engineers. The Museum of Television and Radio's bookshop, library, and tapes were also valuable resources. Much of this book owes its success to the Internet, where hundreds of articles, sound files, and historical background information are easily accessible. In every case, I have tried to do due diligence to the people, agencies, clients, and commercials.

Obviously, one of the hardest tasks in writing this book was choosing which campaigns to include. After all, selecting the "best commercials over the last half century" calls for judgment. Over the past 50 years, there have been literally tens of thousands of radio commercials. There have been innumerable spots created by copywriters and producers at hundreds of advertising agencies, many award-winning and sales-producing, many forgotten a moment after they aired. Because radio is a regional and local medium and one that can target specific audiences through specialized station formats, I'm sure there are many radio commercials that belong in this book that I've never heard. There are many commercials that I do remember that aren't in this collection, like the hilarious campaign created by Walt Kramer for Fotomat in the sixties featuring crazed Christmas elves. As I recall, this series of pre- and postholiday commercials had a group of wild elves with speeded-up voices offering to help customers get their Christmas photos processed faster through a chain of Fotomat kiosks that promised a two-day turnaround.

Another campaign that belongs in this collection, but one I couldn't include because of my inability to reach the people associated with the campaign, is the series of breakthrough spots for Cadbury Callard & Bowser Toffees that were created for the Lord, Geller, Federico, Einstein agency in the early eighties with Monty Python founder and actor John Cleese. Although ad agencies have used and continue to use recognizable comedians and movie stars, Cleese brought his own unique style to pitching these imported English toffees in six commercials that ran in 1982. The spots, which garnered many awards and appeared in the 1982 *Communication Arts* annual, were created by Lynn Stiles, from LGFE, along with Cleese. Lending his British eccentricity to the decidedly English product, Cleese is so enraptured by the candy that he forgets to mention the product name in the first spot; he then goes on, in the second spot, to apologize for his oversight in the first one and almost fails to mention the product name again! In another of the ads, Cleese works to create some recognition for the Callard and Bowser name through a wickedly arcane mnemonic that is meant to be easy to remember—but therein lies the joke. Cleese tells the listener to remember "Cal-" as in "Cal-vin Coolidge," "-lard" as in "Jess Wil-lard," "and" as in "Hans Christian Anderson," "Bow-" as in "Bau-haus" . . . and so on.

I chose the campaigns included here for some very practical as well as personal reasons. First, I chose what stuck in my head as the most truly classic spots. Radio being an ephemeral medium, I wanted to include the commercials that had demonstrated longevity. In some cases, I had a personal preference for a campaign that showcased its creator's talent. For instance, even though Mal Sharpe had conducted thousands and thousands of hours of man-on-the-street interviews and turned them into zany commercials, I wanted his first *paid* commercials for Bell Brand potato chips because they represented his successful foray into advertising. In the case of Dick and Bert, I chose the *Time* magazine campaign because it was the spark that launched their success to a broader range of clients and introduced a style of advertising that has since become classic.

Second, as a practical matter, many recordings of the original commercials no longer exist. Although some production companies do maintain archives, storage space at ad agencies is often at a premium. Thirty-year-old radio commercials on reel-to-reel tape and audiocassettes usually get thrown out. The high turnover rate of agency personnel means there's often no one to keep track of the archives. When I visited Bert Berdis in his offices on Cahuenga Boulevard in Hollywood, he had to rummage around in a cabinet to find a cassette with the *Time* magazine commercials on it. Joy Golden dug into her closet in her studio apartment to find a tape of her 20-year-old Laughing Cow cheese commercials. And Mal Sharpe had to open dusty boxes of quarter-inch reel-to-reel tape to make a CD of his 40-year-old Bell Brand potato chip campaign. Unless you are able to market your old commercials like Stan Freberg or Bob and Ray to nostalgia buffs, it can be a challenge to locate the material.

I had to choose only campaigns that I felt demonstrated groundbreaking innovation, mastery of the medium, award-winning fame, and enduring scope. Among them, Freberg's Contadina tomato paste spots broke the radio comedy barrier; Golden's Laughing Cow cheese commercials are superb examples of how to create a character with the right words and actors; Mal Sharpe's street interviews took radio to a new location; The Richards Group made Motel 6 and Tom Bodett one of the longest-running ad campaigns ever created; and April Winchell walked away with big advertising awards for killing little bugs in her spots for Ortho Fire Ant Killer.

To all those other radio commercials that should be here, I only wish I had the time and space to feature you.

They only last for 60 seconds, but people remember them for decades. That's what makes them great. And now, a few laughs from our sponsor. . . .

Acknowledgments

There are many people I wish to thank for their assistance and generosity in helping me complete this book: Gerry Sindell for his initial guidance in preparing my proposal and his early encouragement; Norm Durkee for his insightful suggestions; Richard Kroll for his invaluable research; and Wendy Frech at the Radio Advertising Bureau. I also thank all the advertising agencies, recording studios, and broadcast services, along with their clients and creative personalities who are themselves the true heroes of the history of radio advertising: Bob Elliott, Stan Freberg, Donovan Freberg (thanks for the phone number!), Mal Sharpe, Dick Orkin, Bert Berdis, Anne Winn, Garrett Brown, Greg Goyne, Eric Studer, Thomas Hripko, Dave Fowler, Tom Faulkner, Rod Underhill, Joy Golden, Richard Costello, April Winchell, Steve Morris, David Lubars, Ken Bennett, Vince Werner, Paul Fey, John Sarley, Dan Price, Mitch Raboy for his superb sound editing . . . and, of course, my editors Airié Dekidjiev and Jessie Noyes for their faith and for answering a rookie's endless questions.

Introduction: Laughter Is Good for Business

The average radio commercial is made up of only 60 seconds' worth of voices, noises, music, and sales messages, and yet the best of them can live in our memories for decades. In fact, over the past 50 years—ever since Jack Benny first joked about sponsors such as Canada Dry, Chevrolet, and Lucky Strike during the broadcasts of his radio programs—radio advertising has used humor to make the copy points memorable and the sponsor's name indelible.

Certainly during more dour times over the past half century, humor was frowned on as being inappropriate for the serious business of sales. Even when the sponsor might be offering a more lighthearted or fun product—such as Jell-O or Piels beer—traditional advertising practitioners felt that the soft-sell approach of using entertaining humor to make a sale less strident would be ineffective.

Time has proven them wrong. Humor is the single largest category for the prestigious Radio-Mercury Awards, sponsored by the Radio Advertising Bureau, a 50-year old industry trade group that promotes radio advertising sales. More radio production companies specialize in creating funny commercials than any other style. Voluminous marketing research over the past 20 years has proven that consumers are more likely to remember something that made them laugh than straight advertising copy. As Dan Price of Oink Ink, one of today's radio advertising production companies, put it, "I'd rather listen to someone who made me laugh than someone who bored me to death." It's a sentiment that has its roots all the way back to one of the founding fathers of modern humorous radio advertising, Stan Freberg.

In the late 1950s, Freberg objected to being "assaulted from his car radio each day" by the hard sell of pushy, obnoxious commercials and sought to create something that people would actually want to hear. He wasn't alone in his objections; ever since commercials began to interrupt radio programs, listeners have been tired of being "sold." Humor has a way of disarming consumers' natural skepticism of advertising in general. Over time, as advertisers grew less traditional and serious and were willing to use humor, their commercials became more entertaining to listen to. Those radio commercials that effectively used comedy in novel ways consistently won awards from advertising professionals, accolades from the public, and most important, increased sales. Those advertising agencies that knew how to tap into the humorous power of radio for their clients spent their budgets wisely.

However, with the advent of television as an advertising medium in the late 1950s, the appeal of radio diminished within many ad agencies. Writing a TV commercial—with its powerful visual appeal, cinematic possibilities, and larger budgets—was far more alluring to agency creative people than writing a mere radio commercial. Radio was usually considered only for clients with small media budgets, geographically dispersed audiences, or a large drive-time commuter target. All of these factors relegated the creative assignments of writing for radio to junior writers. It became a more specialized task as the medium of radio was recommended less and less in favor of television. Certainly today, there are exceptions, as a number of ad agencies understand how to create award-winning, sales-generating radio—DDB Chicago with its work for Anheuser-Busch Bud Light beer; Goodby, Silverstein & Partners for Hewlett-Packard and Budweiser beer; Cliff Freeman & Partners for Hollywood Video and Little Caesar pizza; and Fallon for Lee Apparel, among others. These ads consistently appear among the top finalists in awards shows, such as the Radio-Mercury Awards.

Historically, however, as radio became a specialized task, agencies would farm out those assignments to creative radio production companies. Dick and Bert, Stan Freberg, Bob and Ray, and Chuck Blore were early luminaries in the industry. Today, the number of creative broadcast boutiques (Oink Ink, Outer Planet, World Wide Wadio, Radio in the Nude, and many others) continues to thrive and attract the specialized creative talent who live, eat, and breathe humorous radio.

Many people influenced the course of humorous radio advertising over the past 50 years. Some, like Stan Freberg, Mal Sharpe, Bob Elliott, and Ray Goulding, were keen observers of popular culture and well-known social satirists who were introduced to radio by savvy advertising professionals. Others, such as Joy Golden, Garrett Brown, and Anne Winn, were copywriters themselves who brought a unique style and approach that set new standards. Still others, including Dick Orkin, Jerry Stiller and Anne Meara, and April Winchell, brought their backgrounds as actors and performers to radio advertising.

Many of the people featured in this book are still actively creating radio commercials. Dick Orkin can be found at his Radio Ranch in Hollywood, while across town in Los Angeles, Bert Berdis and Company continue to craft funny commercials. Stiller and Meara are busy in movie, television, and stage careers, but can be heard from time to time when they've been coaxed back into a recording studio. Joy Golden is at her Joy Radio, Inc., in Manhattan, and Mal Sharpe resides in Berkeley, California. Others are tougher to find. To reach Stan Freberg, who still works dervishly at his art, I had to contact him through his son, Donovan, a voice-over actor himself. And the web site for Radio Savant, April Winchell's production company, has no telephone number, only a web address, so I had to e-mail her. I contacted the venerable Bob Elliott of Bob & Ray through the mail, sending a letter to him at his country house in Maine, and received a couple of perfectly quirky missives from him. Contacts for all these folks can be found at the end of the book.

And Now a Few Laughs from Our Sponsor explores some of the funniest and most memorable radio campaigns of the past five decades. Freberg's seminal spots for Contadina tomato paste are here, as are a couple of selections from Bob & Ray for Piels beer. Stiller and Meara are represented by their commercials for Blue Nun wine. And among the many, many commercials Dick Orkin and Bert Berdis created, the spots for *Time* magazine show off their artistry to optimal effect. The chatty, provocative banter between "that laughing woman" Anne Winn and the "smooth guy" Garrett Brown for Molson beer has its own chapter. And some of the new practitioners creating today's award-winning spots can also be found in the last chapter.

Each chapter takes an insider's look at the radio advertising gems and the creative geniuses who conceived them. Because radio is a temporal medium, with its sound disappearing into the ether of our mind's ears over time, this book seeks to capture the stories, techniques, and personalities that are part of a legacy in marketing communications through firsthand interviews, radio scripts, inside anecdotes, and news articles.

Because comedy is contextual, each chapter attempts to place the commercials in their historical and social settings to better explain why the jokes worked. This historical approach should help readers—and listeners—understand the relevance of these commercials. Knowing what was going on in a radio news broadcast around the featured commercials should help today's readers see the context of the commercial and appreciate its humor. Freberg's jingle for Contadina, which *doesn't* mention the product name until the last second, flew in the face of hundreds of mindless on-air jingles that endlessly repeated a product's brand. The simple honesty of Tom Bodett for Motel 6's economy lodging stands in Spartan contrast to the big-budget musical production numbers of the 1980s from its hospitality competition. Bob & Ray's quirky scenarios for Piels beer co-opted current events of the late 1950s to make the fictional fraternals seem all the more real. And the macabre glee of killing fire ants in the Ortho insecticide commercials created by Radio Savant thumbs its nose at the political correctness of today's groups such as PETA.

My goal in writing *And Now a Few Laughs from Our Sponsor* is to appeal to anyone who has ever chuckled out loud over a radio commercial, and to preserve the best moments from a medium that's part of our cultural consciousness. The funny routines, silly characters, comedy sketches, and humorous slogans will tickle the memories and evoke a nostalgic smile. The book is also a valuable tool for people who create radio advertising for a living. At the end of each chapter are practical lessons drawn from the writers, engineers, and creative people who were responsible for the commercials included in the book. You'll find tips on casting the right actors, writing humorous copy, breaking the media clutter, working with sound designers and engineers, sharpening creative skills, directing voice-over talent, and other helpful ideas from the masters.

Whether you're a copywriter, a student of advertising, or a broadcast producer, this look into the minds of the people who have made radio advertising history offers a fresh, real-world perspective on a highly specialized—and lively—craft.

① When Advertising First Got Funny

Today, humor is an integral part of advertising. It's almost impossible to listen to the radio or watch television for more than an hour without encountering at least one commercial that uses humor to deliver its sales message.

Whether the jokes in today's commercial are skillfully integrated into a story that's part of the commercial's concept or spoken by a comedic announcer, over 30 studies in marketing literature have examined the effects of comedy in advertising and determined that humor is one of the most commonly employed communication strategies. According to one paper published in *The Journal of Advertising Research* in May 1995, researchers estimated that 30 percent of all radio advertising used humor. That same article cited a survey conducted in 1984 among advertising research and creative executives in the top 150 U.S. ad agencies in which radio was found to be the best medium (contrasted to television, print, and outdoor) for using humor. The study also determined that there was increased recall of both the subject and the execution when humor was used in a radio commercial. Findings in the study also concluded that the use of humor *unrelated* to the subject and used only to grab attention was a risky strategy.

What advertising researchers have confirmed in pages and

pages of analysis, creative people have always known instinctively: Humor, when used appropriately, can increase the recall of advertising messages, raise the level of favorability toward the ad, and improve the impact of the ad among its target audiences.

In an article that appeared in *Back Stage* magazine in September 1989, journalist Arden Dale asked a group of advertising creative directors their opinions about humor in ads. They concurred that "really funny advertising was scarce," that "most attempted ad humor failed," and that for humor to be successful it must be "rooted strongly in a concept" related to the product. According to the creatives who were in the discussion, the airwaves were "clogged with people trying to be funny and failing." The same issues that researchers noted—relevancy, appropriateness, risk taking, and recall—were played back by the people responsible for creating and approving funny commercials. Said David Fowler, the creative director responsible for the humorous Motel 6 campaign, "What better thing to give the audience than a couple of laughs on behalf of your client?"

But radio commercials weren't always allowed to be funny. Throughout its history—from the medium's early beginnings in the late 1920s until the early 1960s—radio advertising was serious business. In the early days of live radio broadcasting, sponsors considered the copy in their commercials to be sacred, untouchable, and strictly business—not funny business. Early radio program sponsors, such as General Foods, American Tobacco, General Motors, Texaco, and Canada Dry, did not broach any humor in their commercials. Actors and announcers in the live radio studio broadcasts had to read the copy *exactly* as it was approved by the sponsor and cleared by network censors. When American Tobacco aired commercials for their various cigarette brands, slogans such as "L/S/M/F/T—Lucky Strike means fine tobacco" and lines like "so round, so firm, so fully packed" were delivered with the utmost seriousness. When two actresses in a radio soap opera discussed their complexions in a radio commercial, they spoke with the seriousness of a grave health problem; when pitching a commercial for Wheaties breakfast cereal, the announcer's audible "smile" was 100 percent wholesome and 0 percent humorous.

Even as late as the mid-1950s, advertising agencies, on behalf of their clients, treated copy as "sacred as the Bill of Rights," according to Stan Freberg, the legendary Father of Funny Radio. There were advertising leaders, such as Claude Hopkins in 1923 and Rosser Reeves in 1960, who asserted that no one would buy anything from a clown. David Ogilvy, founder of Ogilvy & Mather, claimed that copywriters should avoid the temptation to entertain using humor (though he changed his mind in the early 1980s). When humor was used in an ad as late as the early 1960s, it was considered risky and dangerous. Humor was a hotly debated topic among critics of advertising in the industry and in the popular press. Humorous approaches were first regarded as groundbreaking when they were successful, and even as humor gained acceptability, it was still confined to "fun" lifestyle products such as beverages, deodorants, and household cleaners. It was only in the late 1970s that humor was acceptable for more serious advertisers, including banks, life insurance, and *Time* magazine.

One reason ads were not humorous had to do with the extreme level of control that agencies exerted over every aspect of the presentation. In the early days of commercial radio, many of the top radio programs were packaged by the leading advertising agencies as single-sponsor vehicles for their major clients (e.g., General Foods, General Motors, Lux Soap). This gave sponsors and their agency representatives tremendous power over everything, from the content and personalities in the shows to the ads. One ad agency producer from Young & Rubicam had to get clearance for every word in every commercial from a vice president at his client company. Naturally, this level of control by the sponsors irked many of the more iconoclastic creative performers. Fred Allen, one of the more famous American radio comedians, compared his sponsors and their agencies to "a bit of executive fungus that forms on a desk that has been exposed to a conference," according to an article in *ASAP* magazine in November 1999. His antipathy toward advertisers and their controlling power often made sponsors and their commercials the target of his jokes. The parodies of advertising agencies he created for his program's Mighty Allen Art Players were some of the funniest, and sharpest, of all his skits. Allen was not afraid of the power of his sponsors and their ad agencies; like Allen, Ed Wynn was also a radio comedian who spoofed his sponsor, Texaco. As the serious announcer read the copy about the service stations and its gasoline, Wynn would often interject, "That so?" and other side comments. Humor made the sponsor more memorable, and Wynn salted his shows with jokes about Texaco and their gas stations wherever he could.

While Wynn and Allen might have joked about their sponsors from time to time, another comedian became known and hailed for the same technique. In fact, if there is any date that marks the moment when radio advertising first became funny, it is 1932, the year that one of the greatest radio comedians, Jack Benny, made fun of his first sponsor, Canada Dry beverages.

According to Milt Josefsberg, in his biography, *The Jack Benny Show: The Life and Times of America's Best Loved Entertainer,* "Jack Benny was . . . the first . . . to kid his sponsor's commercials by making them humorous and integrating them into the body of the script" (Josefsberg, p. 321). Prior to Benny, comedians and radio shows would stop the story line and jokes for the sponsors' commercials. Media critic Leonard Maltin wrote in *The Great American Broadcast* that on the comedy program, *The Fibber McGee and Molly Show,* "announcer Harlow Wilcox would suddenly—and peremptorily—appear in the midst of the week's story, and though he was not a character in the town of Wistful Vista, Fibber or Molly would engage him in a conversation that would lead to a message for Johnson's wax . . ." (Maltin, p. 161).

Benny's genius was that he "conceived his comedy offerings with continuity as a dominating factor . . . and . . . popularized . . . the comedy commercial," wrote Josefsberg. Benny's style of comedy was based on what we now think of as situation comedies, in which the comedy is integral to the context of the story, rather than the vaudevillian routines that were translated from the stage to the radio studio. To maintain that continuity, Benny insisted that his staff of writers incorporate his sponsors' names and products as jokes into the body of his show.

The first time Benny did this was for his first radio sponsor, Canada Dry, the giant beverage bottler. By today's standards, the joke is quite tame. Benny read a telegram that reportedly came from a representative of Canada Dry who'd found eight tourists lost in the Sahara Desert without water for a month. The soft drink rep rescued the tourists, giving them each a glass of Canada Dry soda pop. "Not one of them didn't like it!" was the punch line.

The audience loved it, as evidenced by letters and fan mail. But after 78 Canada Dry–sponsored shows with huge audience ratings, the sponsor canceled Benny's contract because it didn't like being the butt of Benny's jokes. Other sponsors clamored to step in and take over the show by 1933. Benny settled on Chevrolet, but after he kidded the car manufacturer in his typical style, someone at Chevrolet objected, and despite a huge audience rating, Benny's contract was not renewed. When the company later realized its mistake, a senior executive at Chevrolet attempted to get Benny back, but General Tire had already signed him. Benny later switched sponsors again, from Jell-O to Grape-Nuts, but he had the audience support and creative savvy to craft a half-hour script about how he'd switched sponsors once more.

Josefsberg notes that ". . . Jack's kidding of the commercials became a high plateau of humor on his programs, and the public looked for it as eagerly as the rest of the show." Rather than thinking of commercials as the cue to leave the room, Benny's listeners eagerly waited each week to see how he would tease his sponsor. It was no small task for Josefsberg or any of Benny's many writers to come up with new ideas each week. They had opera singers pitch a product's selling points in satirical arias. They wrote commercials in phony Shakespearean language and had dramatic actors read them. Benny incorporated jokes about his hefty announcer sidekick, Don Wilson, by referring to his girth as the six flavors of Jell-O (alluding to one of Benny's most famous and highly recognized long-running sponsors). Benny's success even earned him the license to spoof one of the most feared and dictatorial sponsors, George Washington Hill, president of American Tobacco Company, with numerous gags about Lucky Strike's famous slogan, *L/S/M/F/T,* "Lucky Strike means fine tobacco," and "Be Happy—Go Lucky!"

To prove that humor had a positive effect, the Young & Rubicam ad agency conducted national research to determine whether listeners could identify the sponsor of the Jack Benny program. Benny's was the only radio show on the air to score a 91 percent immediate sponsor recall—a record that had never been bested. It was proof that humor was a powerful tool in helping sponsors communicate their message.

In her biography of her husband, *Jack Benny,* Mary Livingstone Benny quoted from an article in *McCall's* magazine in which the Algonquin Hotel Round Table pundit and writer Heywood Broun wrote that radio audiences were becoming sullen about advertising interruptions to programs and that the American sense of humor wouldn't stand for the awed reverence with which announcers spoke the names of the products they were advertising. Broun ended the article by hoping that "in the days to come a grateful people would erect a statue to Jack Benny, with the simple inscription: 'In memory of the first man to take the curse off radio commercials!' " (Benny, p. 59).

Benny established a precedent for using humor in an appropriate context for radio advertising. Other radio personalities from the 1930s and 1940s—including Fred Allen, Arthur Godfrey, and Harry Morgan—also began to add humor to the sponsors' messages on their programs. Though it has taken more than half a century to make humor a mainstream tool for radio advertising, radio copywriters everywhere owe a debt of gratitude to Jack Benny.

② Piels Beer: The Fresh and Timely Humor of Bob and Ray

Client: Piel Brothers Beer

Agency: Young & Rubicam

Production Company: Goulding-Elliott-Greybar Productions, Inc.

Date: 1956–1963

I t can be honestly said that the first names in *recorded* funny radio advertising were Bob and Ray. The advertising campaign that radio personalities Bob Elliott and Ray Goulding created for Piel Brothers beer ran on and off from 1956 to 1963; it set the standard for the soft-sell, highly creative radio commercial that was to become a mainstay of contemporary advertising. Although the Piels campaign was best known for its innovative use of animated television characters to depict the fictitious Bert and Harry Piel brothers, Bob and Ray remained true to their roots in radio by not only doing the characters' voices, but by creating radio commercials as part of the integrated Piels campaign. Even almost half a century later, the radio campaign is a lesson in simplicity, topicality, and vitality.

Anyone who has ever studied the history of radio comedy is no doubt familiar with the silly cast of oddball characters created and voiced by Bob Elliott and Ray Goulding. During their 40-plus year career of "slapstick parody, verbal nonsense, non sequitur and sheer wit" that Whitney Balliett described in his 1973 *New Yorker* profile, the two "strangely gifted New Englanders" added a new dimension to radio. From their conventional beginnings in 1946 as a disk jockey and a newscaster at Boston's WHDH radio station, Bob and Ray took the traditions of broadcasting and turned them upside down. Their gentle form of humor—never blue, never cruel, always strange—helped Bob and Ray become a social and entertainment phenomenon of their day. Wildly popular in Boston and New York, and later across the entire country, Bob and Ray virtually invented the genre of humorous personality radio. When the duo first entered the New York market, they competed with local radio personalities Gene Rayburn (later of the *Match Game* on TV) and Dee Finch, another New York mainstay. But within weeks the competitions' ratings began to drop. Thanks to Bob and Ray, a new kind of comedy was on the air.

In the course of their 15-minute and weekly one-hour radio shows broadcast in New York and on the NBC national radio network, Bob and Ray often ad-libbed their way through character comedy that included spoofs of the radio medium itself—from pathetic interviews and mindless remote broadcasts to incomprehensible field reports and bogus commercials.

As Bob Elliott remembered, Ray and he were doing a daily three-hour morning radio show on New York radio station WINS in 1955, structured around "a few records, news, weather, sports . . . and the characters we'd built up by that time." They were also doing clever commercials for ridiculous fictitious products and businesses that parodied all the conventions of advertising of the day—from Brand X comparisons to unbelievable testimonials to patently unnecessary goods with mindless slogans such as, "Do you inhale when you smoke ham?" Make-believe clients such as Kretchford Braid and Tassel, New England Doll and Novelty, Whippet Motor Car Company, and Einbinder Flypaper were regular sponsors on Bob and Ray shows. It was only fitting that the two should knock their sponsors, real or otherwise, following the precedent of Jack Benny, Fred Allen, and Henry Morgan, all of whom often joked about their sponsors in the 1940s.

But the joke was really a kind of gallows humor in 1955 as advertisers flocked to the new medium of television, all but abandoning radio as a viable advertising vehicle. Radio comedians like Benny saw nearly half their audience drop off as people switched to the medium of television. However, Bob and Ray had developed such a huge following with their own brand of humor that they continued to attract attention.

Fortunately for the Piel Brothers brewers in Brooklyn, one of the radio devotees was a 26-year-old copywriter named Ed Graham Jr., who was working on the Piel's account at the Young & Rubicam advertising agency.

Graham was a big fan of Bob and Ray, and, as Elliott recalled, the young copywriter would drop by the studios to sit in on their morning antics on his way to work. The WINS studio on 28 West 44th Street in Manhattan was located just a few blocks away from Y&R, which is on Madison between 41st and 40th Streets. The friendship between them grew and with it, Elliott said, "hints from Ed that he had an idea for a commercial series that he was attempting to persuade his agency to go along with."

Piels had been one of the surviving local brews from a long-standing number of beer producers—including Ballantine, Rheingold, and Schaeffer—that were brewed with the soft water in the Bushwick area of Brooklyn. In the mid-1950s, wrote Jay Maeder in a 1998 *Daily News* article, Piel Brothers was selling around a million barrels a year as a popularly priced regional brand for the working class. At the time, Y&R was running a campaign that stressed what is now called the "low-calorie" benefits of Piels beer. The marketing strategy had been focused on the hard-sell approach, touting empirical evidence that demonstrated the less fattening quality of the poor-tasting brew. Graham knew that the beer needed something more to make it stand out from its competition.

In an era when the hard sell was the only sell that advertisers and agencies knew, a soft-sell approach was seen as a waste of a client's money. Rosser Reeves, the no-nonsense copywriter who eventually became chairman of Ted Bates & Company ad agency, was the leading proponent of hard-sell advertising. Reeves did not believe in entertaining consumers; he used simple, attention-getting devices and repeated a single sales message over and over again. One of the most famous examples is his early television commercial for Anacin pain reliever that showed animated hammers and lightning bolts representing different types of headaches that Anacin could cure. He wasn't alone in disdaining softer, or more "original," creative ads. In fact, articles in many business magazines derided the "creative" soft-sell approach that threatened long-standing advertising institutions. When Graham championed the soft-sell approach it was a rather radical departure from the tried-and-true. The way Reeves and other advertising figures at the time hammered home their single-minded, unique selling propositions was more in keeping with the monolithic conservatism of Eisenhower, the cold war and 1950s conformity. In 1956, Pepsodent toothpaste introduced its hard-sell jingle, "You'll wonder where the yellow went when you brush your teeth with Pepsodent," choosy mothers were urged to choose JIF peanut butter, and Dash laundry detergent got clothes cleaner than any other product especially made for automatic washers.

In contrast, Graham believed he could bring a softer sell to Piels beer and attract attention for the middle-market brand. Though the Piels commercials may have been soft-selling the beer through the Bert and Harry routines, Bob and Ray were actually only the performers for commercials. Based on his regular visits to Bob and Ray studio performances, Graham had a very good understanding of their style of humor. He knew that he could write scripts for their voices and humor using the characters of Bert and Harry Piel that he'd created. "Ed wrote the copy, and we polished it up to our style," Elliott recalled.

To help him create the characters of Bert and Harry Piel, Graham crafted entire personality profiles for the two make-believe brothers. No less a literary figure than *New York Times* writer Brooks Atkinson included in a column in November

1960 the "personal histories" of the brothers Piel. The two were a study in contrast: Bert, played by Goulding, was a "gabby, obnoxious super salesman who shouted his commercials, scolded the audience and . . . squelched . . . hesitant Harry," played by Elliott, as reported in a May 1956 *Time* magazine article titled "Spiel for Piel." Graham had Bert and Harry growing up in Flatbush, Brooklyn—not too far from the real-life brewery. He gave Bert a wife and son and made Harry a bachelor chemist who discovered "a colloidal suspension which causes cellulose to congeal" that was the purported formula for brewing the dry Piels beer. Graham even gave Bert a fictional career move as eastern sales manager for the Graham-Paige Motor Car company—the same type of silly, fake company that Bob and Ray spoofed on their radio program. Indeed, Graham could imitate Bob and Ray almost as well as they did in their improvisational cast of erratic characters on their shows.

When Graham began to work up the concept of the Piel brothers, he conceived a full campaign—radio, newspaper, and the new medium of television. His art director partner, Jack Sidebotham, created the two cartoon characters who would later be animated for television by the UPA studio, the same animation firm that developed Mr. Magoo, the nearsighted curmudgeon, and the Oscar award–winning, sound-effects-spouting kid, Gerald McBoingBoing, earlier in 1951. Graham envisioned using 20- and 60-second spots for TV, and the traditional 60 seconds for the standard radio commercials. Piel Brothers was committed to a big media budget to give the campaign high visibility in the eastern United States.

Elliott remembered that one Y&R account executive who was skeptical of the entire soft-sell approach said if it worked, he'd quit. It was a promise he must have had to keep. Graham stuck to his convictions and pitched the campaign idea to the agency and the client. Finally, he got Piel Brothers to test the campaign in Harrisburg, Pennsylvania, and Binghamton, New York.

Bob and Ray and Graham's campaign for Piel's was, as

Elliott put it, "tritefully, an overnight success." Not only did the campaign attract a huge audience that was willing to buy the beer, but it also propelled Bob and Ray into a new sideline venture when they formed Goulding-Elliott-Graham Productions to produce the radio and television commercials for Piel's and, eventually, other clients.

Even though advertising history focuses on the animated Piels television commercials that Bob and Ray voiced, the radio commercials were equally important, and in the early 1950s when television was in its infancy, television commercials were, in fact, virtually radio commercials with pictures. The animated Bert and Harry Piel visually depicted the characters that Bob and Ray had been creating on radio. So convincing were their personifications that tens of thousands of people assumed they were the real Piel brothers behind the beer. In a weird twist of fate that plagued Elliott and Goulding for years, people would see them in public and call them Bert and Harry. As Elliott put it simply, "We hated that . . . it got under our skins."

Typical of the commercials that Graham wrote for Bob and Ray were the fussy fights between Bert, with his blustery sales tactics, and Harry, the levelheaded one. As would be the case with many a long-running campaign, there was always a need to refresh the commercials to keep the advertising current. The running gag was that Bert was constantly cooking up wild ad schemes, while Harry, ever the chemist, tried to improve the beer. Graham's spots would often use topical humor, such as a parody of the Russian industrial tours of U.S. factories popular in the mid-1950s. A series of spots hawks the product claiming that the foamy head on a Piels beer seals in flavor. As Elliott remembered, breweries were always changing marketing strategies: "One year it might be cold-brewed and the next oven-brewed." Among the commercials Bob and Ray did was one that made fun of the typical radio remote broadcast from the steps of the brewery as Bert tried to demonstrate to passersby just how long the head lasted on a glass of Piels beer. Many of the commercials involved the kind of self-referential advertising that Bob and Ray were spoofing on their radio show. In one spot, a fictitious Eugene Hill, representing Brand X beer, bursts into the recording studio as Harry and Bert are making a commercial. Hill demands equal time to sell his two-year-old, poor-tasting brew. "Ladies and gentlemen," Hill pleads, "Brand X may not have a long-lasting head. It may not taste as good as Piels, but . . ." he chokes up here, "we're doing the best we can." The interruption of the Piels commercial continues when Hill apologizes for the inferior quality of Brand X beer because Piels "has been at this thing longer." The mayhem escalates when he asks if every beer has to be as good as Piels and the brothers each take an arm and throw him out of the studio. "Sob sister!" Bert shouts after him. The spot cleverly worked in the copy points, not by the typical hard sell, but by taking a comparative perspective with the straw man of Brand X; the approach was highly unusual for the time because it dared to make fun of a competitor, albeit a phony one.

In another spot, Bob and Ray traded on the topicality of a Russian industrialist touring an American factory, spoofing the Kruschevian visits to American industries that made headlines in the late fifties. In the commercial, Bob and Ray rapidly switch back and forth as they act out the entire cast of characters—almost simultaneously playing a Russian brewer with a Communist five-year plan, his inept translator, and Bert and Harry Piel. In an era when radio production didn't have the technical benefit of overdubbing multiple voices, the commercial is a vocal quick-change extravaganza. The copy points were artfully integrated into the silliness rather than shoved into the listener's ear. The Russian, through his translator, asks, "Regarding the head on your Piels beer, which lasts so long and therefore keeps flavor and life . . ."—and then the translator corrects himself—"uh, *freshness* from escaping, how can I instruct my breweries back home to imitate Piels beer and create a beer of our own exactly similar to it?"

With typical bellicosity, Bert tells the Russian flatly, "Ya can't!" The spot dissolves into a parody of cold war posturing; the Russian claims that in five years (then the standard Soviet industrial planning period) he can make his beer as good as Piels.

In another commercial that linked the Piels radio and television campaign, Bert is standing on the steps of his brewery, hawking the long-lasting head on Piels through a loudspeaker. After standing outside all day because the head lasted so long, Bert tells the crowd that "the head is still there but we are taking it inside now. . . . But we're thinking of you. We don't want you to miss your buses." It's the kind of gentle yet sarcastic humor that gave Bob and Ray material its gentle bite. In the spot, there's a great throwaway line, spoken by someone in the crowd—most likely voiced by Elliott—who says that Bert looks a lot younger than he does on TV. It's an almost surrealistic mirror of self-referential advertising.

To ensure the campaign would be a success, Piel Brothers committed to a large media budget, and Bob and Ray found themselves in their recording studio two to three times a week recording new spots. It was the media phenomenon of the time, and the campaign was reviewed in numerous newspapers and magazines. Further proof of the success of the campaign appeared in a May 1956 *Time* magazine article reporting that interest in the Piels beer commercials was so high that Y&R had to print the media schedule in the newspaper to inform people when the spots would appear. Bert and Harry Piel fan clubs boasted "millions" of members. Publicity for the campaign was, no doubt, part real and part orchestrated public relations carried out by Y&R itself. The campaign succeeded, and by 1956, Piels sales had gone up 21 percent.

People loved Bert and Harry; unfortunately, they didn't love the beer. Reported Lenore Skenazy in a 1987 *Advertising Age* article, "Piels beer was so bad that the more people tried it, the faster word spread of its foul taste—thus proving (perhaps for the first time): Nothing kills a bad product faster than good advertising." As Elliott remembered ironically, "I'm not and never was a beer connoisseur, but everybody said that they bought it out of loyalty after discovering they didn't like it." The marketing strategy became very clear: resale.

Despite the rampant success of the ads, it wasn't only the bad taste of the beer that marked a decline in sales four years later. A cold summer in the New York area in 1960 added to flattened beer sales. Trying to avert blame for lagging sales, Young & Rubicam started to question the effectiveness of the popular campaign in October and December of that year. Acting fearfully, Y&R lobbied hard to dump the campaign—despite reluctance by the Piel Brothers client. However, the agency's efforts were successful. In December of that year, the *New York Times* reported that contract negotiations between "Piel Brothers and the Goulding-Elliott-Graham Production, Inc., will expire at the end of the year." It looked like the end of Bert and Harry; however, Y&R was faced with a public relations dilemma as they sought to retire the hugely popular characters. It was an example of a campaign that had gained so much popularity that its cancellation would disappoint many people. One article even questioned whether the cancellation of Bert and Harry Piel symbolized the end of the "whole offbeat approach to advertising," or "a general retreat and a return to the hard sell." But the campaign was terminated by 1961. Y&R replaced the Piel brothers with an innocuous jingle celebrating "the glorious Piels . . . the beer with the long-lasting head . . . and glorious crown . . . it holds the flavor all the way down." Ironically, Bob and Ray were replaced with the same kind of jingle they had parodied throughout their radio show career.

But Bob and Ray and Graham had created such enduring characters that after only two years, Y&R was forced by a huge lobbying effort on the part of the public to bring back Bert and Harry Piel. Rather than ignore the valuable equity in the characters, Y&R resurrected the Piel brothers campaign in 1962, but only temporarily. By 1964, the ads were a goner, and the combination of declining sales and the eventual purchase of Piels by the competing brand Schaeffer severed the ties between Y&R and Piels. In an interesting footnote, the Piels brand was handled in 1975 by the Papert Koenig agency in New York, which brought back Bob and Ray to re-create Bert and Harry again for a short while. Intermittently over the next 10 years Bert and Harry were trotted out—in 1983 the Wyse Agency in Cleveland picked up the Piels brand as part of its assignment from the Stroh Brewery, the new owners of the Piels trademark. Wyse created radio commercials commemorating the 100th anniversary of the founding of both Piels and the Brooklyn Bridge, and Bob and Ray were given cameo roles at the end of the new Piels radio commercials as Bert and Harry. The campaign broke in the spring of 1983, ran shortly, and that was the last the public ever heard from Bert and Harry Piel as professional pitchmen. Bob and Ray continued to perform on the air and off, but Ray Goulding passed away in 1990. Elliott continues to comment from time to time on the radio.

When interviewed, Elliott demurred modestly that it was Graham who helped Goulding and him learn to be better advertisers. Some of the lessons that Graham imparted in 1956 are just as valid today.

1. Keep it simple.

"Graham had a rule," Elliott recalled, "if you only had 15 words to sell your product, what would they be?" For radio, it's a fundamental lesson. **Given that a radio commercial is usually 60 seconds long, and the average number of words that can be spoken clearly in that period is 120—simplicity is the rule.** With 15 key words for the copy points, it leaves just enough to create the humorous scene around the message. "The theory was, the shorter you could make the message, the entertainment would be remembered along with the message," said Elliott. Far too often in radio, young copywriters, zealous account executives, or pushy clients want to cram too many claims and copy points into the spot, creating wall-to-wall words. Far from being believable, a fact-filled and overly complex commercial isn't interesting to listen to or even remotely memorable. The 15 words that Bob and Ray chose to put into their commercials were well chosen and important. "It's a hard job," said Elliott, "but someone had to do it."

2. Make it newsworthy.

Advertising does well to incorporate news and current events. Consider the positive impact of putting "new and improved" on any product; it can stimulate sales and provide something to talk about in advertising. Bob and Ray knew this as well as Graham. "There was a big period when one of the congressional investigations [the McCarthy hearings] was going on, and we interviewed this guy coming out of the hearing after being on the stand all day to find out how thirsty he was." In addition, Soviet Premier Nikita Khrushchev's tour of the United States that included a visit to a General Motors plant also offered fodder for Bob and Ray. **Topicality enlivens a commercial by bringing to bear current emotions, sentiments, and references that connect the listener instantly with the message. The trick, of course, is to make sure that the commercial doesn't continue to air long after the event is forgotten.**

3. Keep it fresh.

The vitality of a long-running campaign depends on both the continuity of the characters and the freshness of their next new situation. Bob and Ray kept the Bert and Harry Piel campaign fresh by constantly inventing new scams and schemes for Bert to pitch and giving Harry's reassuringly grounded responses. Keeping the commercials fresh, almost reinventing them each time, was close to the kind of live ad-libbing at which Bob and

Ray excelled as performers. Bob and Ray knew the value of spontaneity. "When we would throw away our prepared script and really ad-lib a spot or two," Elliott said, "the audience was much more with us than when they knew we had been reading prepared stuff." **A commercial that sounds real and freshly conceived—even after it's been played a number of times—is a commercial that will connect with its audience. Avoid trite situations, surprise your listeners, and keep them in suspense. Be as fresh as a glass of Piels, thanks to its long-lasting head.**

Piels Beer
Scripts © Goulding-Elliott-Greybar Productions, Inc.

SFX: [*Knock/knock/knock*]

SFX: [*Door opens*]

ANNCR: You two fellows Bert and Harry Piel?

BERT: Yes we are.

HARRY: Yes we are.

BERT: We're doing a commercial right now.

ANNCR: Eugene Hill. I represent the Brand X brewery. Sirs, we demand equal time.

BERT: Equal . . . ?

HARRY: Equal? This is ridiculous.

BERT: We don't even talk about Brand X anymore. This year we're concentrating on Piels long-lasting head and how it makes our beer extra refreshing.

EUGENE: I understand.

BERT: You see, Piels long-lasting head acts as a seal and it keeps flavor and freshness from escaping.

EUGENE: Are you all through?

BERT: Well, yes.

HARRY: Well, yes.

EUGENE: Ladies and gentlemen, Brand X may not have a long-lasting head. It may not taste as good as Piels. But [*weepy*] we're doing the best we can.

BERT: Well, sir, don't tell us your hard luck.

EUGENE: We've come a long way in the last two years. Naturally, Piels tastes best.

BERT: All right, come on . . .

EUGENE: They've been at this thing longer.

BERT: Show him the way out.

EUGENE: We're only beginners. But does every beer have to be as good as Piels?

BERT: Right this way . . .

EUGENE: No, no there's room for a second best.

HARRY: You take that arm, Bert.

BERT: Come on, you.

SFX: [*Scuffle*]

BERT: Sob sister!

Piels Beer
Scripts © Goulding-Elliott-Greybar Productions, Inc.

RUSSIAN-SPEAKING MAN: [*Speaking in Russian*]

TRANSLATOR: He wishes to know why your Piels beer tastes better than that of other American breweries.

BERT: Tell 'em, Harry.

HARRY: Well, uh, Piels Brothers, here in Brooklyn and Staten Island . . .

BERT: Brew a beer with extra long lasting . . .

HARRY: . . . brew a beer with an extra long lasting head and that head acts like a seal keeping flavor and . . .

BERT: Freshness . . .

HARRY: . . . freshness from escaping.

RUSSIAN SPEAKER: [*Asks question*]

TRANSLATOR: Regarding the head on your Piels beer which lasts so long and therefore keeps flavor and life . . .

RUSSIAN: [*Interrupts and corrects*]

TRANSLATOR: . . . uh, freshness from escaping, how can I instruct my breweries back home to imitate Piels beer and create a beer of our own exactly similar to it?

BERT: Ya can't. It's impossible.

RUSSIAN: [*Talking/arguing with the translator*]

TRANSLATOR: He says, give me five years and I will do it! Do you wish to bet?

BERT: Yes, yes, put your money where your mouth is!

③ Contadina Tomato Paste: Stan Freberg Takes Comedy Seriously

Client: Contadina

Agency: Brisacker-Wheeler

Production Company: Stan Freberg

Date: 1957–1958

During Stan Freberg's half century of brilliant work, he has been called everything from "The Che Guevara of Advertising" by the *New York Times* to "a marketing genius" by *Broadcasting* magazine to a "National Treasure" by the *Los Angeles Times* to a Stradivarius in the symphony of comic voices. Over his long career, Freberg has been hailed as a genius for his records, satire, writing, directing, voice-over acting, composing and lyrics, radio commentary, and advertising. *Advertising Age* cited his contributions to the creative revolution in advertising, proclaiming him "The Father of the Funny Commercial." His advertising awards include 21 Clios, two prestigious Silver Lions from Cannes, and the Orson Welles Award from the Radio Advertising Bureau, to name just a few. His work in advertising, specifically his first advertising assignment ever for Contadina tomato paste, established standards for honesty, objectivity, iconoclasm, and conviction that hold true today.

The radio campaign for Contadina was created for the San Francisco advertising agency, Brisacker-Wheeler in 1957 under the creative direction of the legendary Howard Gossage. The spots aired in 1957 and 1958, according to press releases in

Advertising Age magazine. Later in 1958, *Advertising Age* voted the Contadina campaign one of the two most outstanding marketing successes of the year.

To appreciate the groundbreaking nature of Freberg's commercials for Contadina in 1957, consider their social and cultural context. By the late fifties, the full bounty of the postwar boom was in bloom. The Korean War had ended. America truly was the "consumer horn of plenty." It seemed that no one went without, that grocery stores had more food, that cars had more chrome, that businesses had more customers; the only thing in short supply was irony. Satirists such as Freberg and Mort Sahl had the tiny franchise on that precious commodity, and where they could sell it, they did, and they stood out in the process. And standing out (getting your product noticed) is the cardinal goal of advertising.

To understand what it took for advertising to stand out in the radio environment of the late 1950s, one only need listen to a typical broadcast air check from that time. Say the year is 1957, and from WICE in Rhode Island to KVA in San Francisco, the dulcet tones of AM radio were filled with the lulling simplicity of the good life sung to the tune of a peppy jingle. The language of fifties' advertising was full of confident boasts, hard-sell claims, and upbeat promises—all delivered with a smile. The recorded commercials and the more frequent live announcer spots of that era were unsophisticated in their production and superficial in their pitches. "Flako" Can't Fail Pie Crust mix "really hits the spot," sang one jingle. In an ad for Kent cigarettes, smokers were urged to "give a carton for a Christmas gift." The typical radio jingle used repetition to emphasize the brand name, as in this ditty for Tide detergent:

> *Tide's in, dirt's out/Tide's in, dirt's out/*
> *Tide gets clothes cleaner than any soap/*
> *T-I-D-E, Tide!*

According to Julliann Sivulka's cultural history of American advertising, *Soap, Sex and Cigarettes,* "with more money to spend . . . consumers could be persuaded . . . to shop excessively . . . to lure people into stores . . . manufacturers invested in a blizzard of . . . ads" (p. 245). But the cracks in this feel-good era of consumerism were beginning to show. In contrast to the mindless hard sell on radio was the reality being broadcast over the same airwaves. It was hard to ignore the Communist missile buildup, the cold war face-offs, the federal troops enforcing integration in Alabama, nuclear arms testing, Sputnik, and volatile Middle East politics. The first public stirrings of rebellion—from the 1957 publication of *On the Road,* Kerouac's chronicle of the Beat generation, to civil rights marches—had begun to shake people's complacency. And if advertising is a barometer of the social zeitgeist, then the iconoclasm of Stan Freberg's popular satirical records was perfectly suited to a new kind of sales pitch. As Freberg said in his autobiography, *It Only Hurts When I Laugh,* his first foray into professional advertising was a radio commercial that not "only didn't take itself too seriously," but was actually something people would want to hear instead of turning it off" (p. 94).

Being different from all the other advertising that was on the air at the time was exactly what Howard Gossage wanted from Freberg. According to Freberg, Gossage, then the creative director of Brisacker-Wheeler advertising agency, said he didn't want the ordinary type of "straight" radio spots. Freberg's own sense of being "assaulted from his car radio each day" by the hard sell of commercials was something that more and more people were feeling. The well-received and popular spoofs of advertising being done by Bob Elliott and Ray Goulding on the East Coast testified to consumers' growing distrust of the hard sell.

Gossage appreciated Freberg's humor from his comedy records and short-lived live television show. He decided to call him to help with one of his clients, Contadina Foods. A California tomato paste packer owned by Chicago-based Bell Canto Foods, Contadina was being overwhelmed on the grocery shelves by Hunt's, the leading tomato product packer. Gossage wanted Freberg to create and produce some radio commercials that would be as "unorthodox" as the rest of Freberg's work.

The Contadina brand name had been known to Americans since World War I, when three Italian immigrant families in New York capitalized on the shortage of imported tomatoes caused by the German maritime blockade of 1914. The company moved to San Jose, California, in 1916 and for the next 47 years was a highly regarded operation, processing nearly 200,000 tons of tomatoes and tomato products annually.

Of the two commercials Freberg created for Contadina, the first drew on his musical background. Thanks to his early musical training, he had been writing, scoring, and directing song parodies for his comedy albums for years. Using his musical talents, Freberg employed his offbeat ironic humor to create a jingle for Contadina that mocked the supercilious hard sell of most musical spots of the time. Instead of endlessly repeating the client's name in the lyrics, Freberg did the unthinkable: He didn't mention the sponsor's name until the final few seconds of the spot. Rather, he focused on a more important point of difference, that Contadina tomato paste was thicker, made so by the equivalent of eight tomatoes in every can.

That product difference that Gossage communicated to Freberg became the hook, or the repetitive lyric, of the jingle. In fact it was the *only* copy point of the entire jingle. Even more dramatically, Freberg—always the contrarian—acknowledged the absence of the client's name by having the announcer "correct" the singers' embarrassing oversight. Freberg wrote the jingle: "Who Puts Eight Great Tomatoes in That Little Bitty Can?" and sang the lyrics himself on the commercial accompanied by the Buddy Cole Jazz Quartet. Quite simple in nature, the lyric repeated the question three times and then, in a stroke of brilliant contrariness, ended not with the sponsor's name, but with the line, "You know who, you know who, you know who!" After an embarrassing pause, the announcer intoned, "In case you don't, it's Contadina tomato paste."

When the radio commercials were first presented to the agency staff, the concepts were immediately questioned by everyone. "Where are the recipes the client wanted demonstrating how to use tomato paste?" the account executives asked Gossage; they were used to the conventional ads at the time that offered product tips to make "ethnic" foods more acceptable in the white-bread fifties. One agency executive asked, "How come he didn't tell how much thicker Contadina is than Hunt's?" (p. 96).

But Freberg knew that boasting that Contadina was thicker than Hunt's would be seen as just another specious claim. Thicker is, after all, a relative comparison. Conjuring the mental image of eight tomatoes being squished into a small tomato paste can was far more evocative. What's more, the teaser device of asking a question with its own mnemonic rhyme—"Who puts *eight great* tomatoes in a *little bitty* can?"—was highly provocative. Listeners were tantalized into wanting to hear who the culprit was. It made the name Contadina all the more important and memorable because it *wasn't* repeated ad nauseum. It was said only once.

The second commercial Freberg created for Contadina featured two characters—Freberg cast himself as a zealous promoter for Contadina who hires a dubious contractor (played by Freberg's friend, Peter Leeds) to place a 300-foot can of Contadina tomato paste on top of the Empire State Building.

Seen in the light of today's exaggerated story-dialogue-format radio commercials, the Empire State Building spot does not appear to be too daring. But given the straitlaced straight-announcer pitch popular in the fifties, the commercial is almost seditious.

Most of the commercial is centered around Freberg trying to convince the workman to do something, if not illegal, certainly in defiance of rules and regulations. He wants him to replace the zeppelin mooring tower at the top of the Empire State Building with a huge, blinking mockup of a can of tomato paste.

"Look," the man says nervously, "have you checked with the Empire State Building people? I mean . . . is it all right with *them?*" he asks a pushy Freberg. And later, "We could be arrested!"

"Wellll,' Stan replies, "there's always somebody working on the building . . . they won't know the difference." Freberg's disobedience and opposition to authority echo the spirit of the times—there's an almost teenage disobedient prank going on here: "Everyone is so busy with their nose to the grindstone, no one will notice if I act out," the commercial seems to say.

In fact, Freberg appears to be acting out when he crafted the ending of the spot. Just as the agency and some of the clients questioned the absence of the list of recipes and uses for Contadina tomato paste in the commercial, Freberg manifested his disgust for their conventionality through the dialogue between his fictional self and the workman.

"Now, don't forget to have the can blink in international Morse code the words, 'There are many delicious uses for Contadina tomato paste,' " Freberg tells the workman. "Wait a minute!" the workman says, "I thought you wanted it to blink 'Eight Great Tomatoes in That Little Bitty Can'? . . . Which do you want?" Perhaps this was Freberg's sassy response to the client fiddling with his tag line.

Most creative people in ad agencies know that selling an edgy and different commercial concept can be difficult, particularly when there is little support within the agency. Freberg was depending on Gossage to help sell the spots. As Freberg recounts it, Gossage insisted on playing it for the Marrici brothers, who owned Contadina, and his staff.

"Everyone hated the commercials. Everyone except the president, Marty Marrici, who happened to be the only one who laughed," reported Freberg (P. 98). Marrici decided to see what the food brokers would say when the commercials were played for them and his salespeople. To a man, they hated them too. But in spite of this negative reception and despite the protest of his staff, Marrici approved the commercials, and Freberg's first radio campaign was on the air.

The commercials were an immediate hit. Familiar with Freberg from his comedy albums, the disc jockeys who played the commercials couldn't stop talking about them. In an advertiser's best-of-all-possible publicity, the DJs talked about the commercials after their allotted 60 seconds, effectively giving Contadina valuable free airtime. The commercials were a big success with consumers, too, and Contadina's sales rose dramatically. While 43-year-old monthly sales figures are hard to come by today, Freberg reported at the time that within three months of the campaign airing, Contadina's biggest competitor, Hunt's, had "cut its price twice, six months later it was giving away to the grocers one free case with every ten in an effort to catch up." The campaign helped Contadina gain market share from Hunt's and surge ahead.

What can today's copywriters learn from Freberg's groundbreaking work? A lot. We can intuit several lessons from Freberg's work and comments.

1. Be honest.
Honesty isn't usually associated with advertising; in fact, surveys of credibility often place advertising professionals at the bottom of the list for telling the truth. Copywriters who find a way to "admit" the reality of the product—even if there is something negative about it such as high cost, poor distribution, or its commodity status—can mine the candor for its humor and reach an audience skeptical of specious claims and promotional boasts.

In 1957, truth wasn't necessarily part of an advertiser's handbook. Wild product claims, faked product photographs, and the ever-ready smile were more common in advertising. That's why Freberg's straightforward honesty stood out. It didn't always win him friends or quick acceptance. In his own words, "serious ad practitioners" of advertising just viewed his work as mostly an irritant.

As a satirist, Freberg's instincts led him to poke his finger into the subject where it would tickle his audience the most. Freberg had an unerring ability to see the truth of a situation and then to unapologetically acknowledge it. Calling attention to a product's weak distribution or to the obviousness of a commodity like tomato paste was well suited to Freberg's ironic sense of humor.

Freberg believed in telling the truth, even when it might seem embarrassing. One campaign he did for Kaiser Aluminum was pegged to the concept that the client's aluminum foil was hard to find and not well distributed. As usual, the spots panicked the midlevel executives, angered a few grocers, but amused the president enough to take a chance. The campaign, as predicted, was a smashing success. **Truth sells.**

2. Don't take advertising too seriously.

Those who have been in advertising long enough have an expression when young, zealous account executives get too serious about the copy of an ad: "It's only advertising. It's not brain surgery." Freberg had the same attitude. Even before he created his own commercials, he spent time in the recording studio as a successful voice-over announcer and actor in other people's commercials. He'd been exposed to many agency people who took themselves and their copy too seriously, acting as if every word of their commercials was "straight from the Bill of Rights."

Freberg would never have been able to mock the conventions of advertising if he subscribed to the sacrosanctity of copy. **The objectivity that good copywriters bring to an assignment keeps them from believing the client's own**

internal propaganda. Not taking the ad too seriously also allows writers to view the commercial from the same distance as a consumer. Don't get too close, folks, or you'll miss the big idea.

3. If you want your commercial to be noticed, break something.

Clutter is advertising's enemy. Too many commercials, too many messages, and too much noise make it more and more difficult for a commercial to reach its intended audience. The first lesson radio copywriters have to learn is that they are responsible for keeping the radio listener from switching stations when a commercial comes on.

The bland and expected, the conventional, and the tried-and-true will no longer cut through the clutter. Researchers say that people are exposed to hundreds of advertising messages every day, so as ad-savvy consumers, we tune out the clutter. **Just as a naughty child will sometimes break something to get parental attention, a copywriter has to break something to have a commercial be noticed. Freberg's "anti-jingle" for Contadina broke the rules of traditional jingles because it didn't mention the product repeatedly—only once, as an announced afterthought.**

4. Believe in your ideas.

Freberg had such conviction that his commercials for Contadina were strategically sound and creatively superior that he was willing to stand up to critics and naysayers at the agency and at the client. Everyone initially hated his commercials, which didn't meet their expectations. They didn't sound like traditional commercials. Had Contadina's president not liked them enough to support them, they never would have aired. Both he and Freberg had the courage to believe in their ideas.

But it's an arrogant fool's errand to defend an ad concept or a commercial that isn't conceptually well grounded and perfectly crafted. **The lesson is that it's fine to believe in your idea. Defend your work with all your conviction, as long as it works.**

In the end, Freberg leaves a legacy of iconoclasm and brilliance that shows that zigging while others are zagging cannot only generate groundbreaking advertising, but can also increase sales, bolster awareness, and make people smile.

Contadina Tomato Paste
"Empire State Building/Who Puts Eight Great
Tomatoes in That Little Bitty Can?"
Used by permission of Freberg, LTD

SFX: [*Wind*]

FREBERG: Now look, you got it straight what we want?

CONTRACTOR: Yeah, I think so. You want me to take off the tower from the Empire State Building . . .

FREBERG: That's right. . . .

CONTRACTOR: . . . and put a three-hundred-foot can of Contadina tomato paste up there.

FREBERG: That's right, in full color.

CONTRACTOR: [*Nervously*] Now, look, Mister, are you sure this is all right? Did you check with the Empire State Building people?

FREBERG: Oh, they won't know the difference. Somebody's always working on the building. You know how it is . . .

CONTRACTOR: Yeah, but that tower was put there to moor zeppelins to.

FREBERG: Look, look, let's be realistic. How many zeppelins have moored there in the last month?

CONTRACTOR: Well . . . not many, not many, but look . . . I don't know if I want to get . . .

FREBERG: You want us . . . to . . .

CONTRACTOR: No . . . I don't want to get involved. . . .

FREBERG: You want us to get another contractor? Is that it? Is that it?

CONTRACTOR: No, I like the job . . . but we could be arrested!

FREBERG: Suppose you let me worry about that, huh?

CONTRACTOR: Okay, we'll start first thing in the morning.

FREBERG: Good, now don't forget to have the can blink in international Morse code the words, "There are many delicious uses for Contadina tomato paste."

CONTRACTOR: Now, wait a minute! I thought you wanted it to blink "Eight Great Tomatoes in That Little Bitty Can?"

FREBERG: Yeah, well . . .

CONTRACTOR: Which do you want?

FREBERG: Let me sleep on it. Okay?

CONTRACTOR: Okay.

MUSIC: [*Up and under*]

SINGER: Who puts eight great tomatoes in that little
bitty can?
    Who puts eight great tomatoes in that little bitty
can?
    Who puts eight great tomatoes in that little bitty
can?
    You know who, you know who, you know who!

MUSIC: [*Out*]

SFX: [*Silence*]

ANNCR: In case you don't, it's Contadina tomato paste.

④ Bell Brand Potato Chips: Mal Sharpe's Interviews Are Fresh, Crisp, and Yummy

Client: Bell Brand Potato Chips

Agency: Honig-Cooper & Harrington

Production Company: Man-On-The-Street Productions

Date: 1968

In 1968, Mal Sharpe stood on the corner of Hollywood Boulevard and Vine Street in Los Angeles and ambushed pedestrians with nothing more than his Uher portable tape recorder, his straight man Ernie Anderson, and a bag of Bell Brand potato chips. For Sharpe, it was the beginning of a successful advertising career, marked by commercials from the offbeat, absurdist humor that he and his former partner in crime, Jim Coyle, had already established earlier in the sixties on the streets of San Francisco. But Sharpe's work for Bell Brand potato chips represented more than a three-year series of silly taste-test radio commercials. The streetwise testimonials were truly an audio testimony to the times. Sharpe's techniques for creating commercials demonstrate the value of flexibility, directness, and inspiration.

If the speakeasy represented the lure of the Roaring Twenties and the coffeehouse was the informal headquarters of the Beat generation, the street was center stage for the sixties. The street was the scene of protest marches and civil demonstrations; populist guerrilla street theater dramatized the revolutionary fervor of the day. Even the physical streets themselves took on magical significance, appearing in song lyrics as part of the popular culture—places like London's Carnaby Street, the Sunset Strip, and San Francisco's Haight and Ashbury. In Los Angeles, the famous Hollywood Boulevard had Grauman's Chinese Theater, Musso & Frank's restaurant, Frederick's of Hollywood lingerie shop, and the memorial sidewalk of stars. The boulevard had seen its glory days by the late sixties and had become a magnet to hippies, runaways, and street people, as well as tourists and local citizens. You could still find remnants of the old Hollywood, with sightings of cowboy actors like Lash LaRue, or the new Hollywood, with characters like health food guru Gypsy Boots. The action was on the street. People knew it, and so did the media.

With the advent of lighter-weight, portable video and audio recording equipment in the early sixties, the excitement, novelty, and humanity of the street could be captured and packaged for mass consumption. Broadcasters could become roving reporters, interviewing people on the street as news was being made, and instantly report from the scene. Images of the 1968 Chicago Democratic convention riots appeared on the nightly newscast as they happened. However, it wasn't only the news reporters who were on the street. Entertainers also took advantage of the technology to be there. Comedians like Steve Allen would duck out the back of his studio in Hollywood and have fun with the real people on the street—a tradition continued today by late-night entertainer Dave Letterman.

With a camera and microphone, a street reporter was an authority figure who could grant a moment of fame and glory to the average citizen. Reporters could elicit real-life testimonials coming from the mouths of real people, and these people became entertainment in their own right.

Early in their careers, Sharpe and Coyle would spoof unsuspecting people on the San Francisco streets with strange requests that turned into miniperformance pieces. They used the license of the street reporter to approach people, but far from being conventional, Sharpe played on people's expectation of seriousness to disarm them with wild, oddball pranks.

According to Scott Simon, host of NPR's *Weekend Edition,* in an interview with Sharpe in 2000, Sharpe and Coyle "were also trying to create a kind of insurrection that brazenly lacked both logic and reason."

The disconnect between the presence of a professional street reporter asking weird questions—offering someone a hypothetical job that would lead to certain death, trying to convince a drunken sailor to appear in a phony bank robbery that threatens to turn real—often led to strange and funny confrontations. Fans of Sharpe and Coyle's early work, such as rock-and-roll poet and wild man Henry Rollins, still relish the twisted humor in those disconnections, which can be heard on archival album compilations.

These elements of humor and absurdity came together in Sharpe's original premise for the Bell Brand potato chip radio campaign. Sharpe and Coyle had created the concept of the taste tests while they were still working together in San Francisco. They had pitched the idea to Jack Calnan, creative director at Honig-Cooper & Harrington, the San Francisco agency that represented Bell Brand, a division of Granny Goose Foods, which distributed the Bell Brand only in Southern California. Despite Calnan's best effort to get the client to buy the concept for the spots, it took three pitches before they were finally accepted.

By that time, Sharpe was working in Los Angeles as a copywriter for Chuck Blore, another legendary, creative, radio producer who is famous in his own right for dozens of musical and comedy commercials. When Calnan called Sharpe with the news that Bell Brand had finally agreed to produce the offbeat campaign, he offered Sharpe a $10,000 fee to produce the spots. Sharpe recalls nearly falling out of his chair—the sum was astronomical for the times.

By then, Bell Brand was one of the leading snack foods distributed in Southern California, competing with its sister brand, Granny Goose, as well as Laura Scudder and Lay's.

Produced in Santa Fe Springs, California, an industrial city southeast of Los Angeles, Bell Brand had a long history of using local media to attract audiences. Promotions co-branded with cartoon series—such as *Crusader Rabbit* and *Beany & Cecil* (coincidentally written and voiced in part by Stan Freberg!)— were part of Bell Brand's legacy from the late fifties. By the late sixties, the potato chip wars were firing up their media guns in Southern California for the lucrative snack foods market. At the time, Bell Brand was running a local ad campaign using television and outdoor billboards that featured a finicky female chip inspector who examined every chip on the assembly line that went into Bell Brand bags.

For personal reasons, Sharpe and Coyle had split up by 1964, and Jim Coyle had gone with his wife to London. Without his longtime friend and partner, Sharpe needed a straight man to work with him on the street when he did his ambush-interview testimonial commercials. He chose Ernie Anderson, a voice-over announcer with a dry, deadpan style who had been a local star in Cleveland radio and television and who had worked alongside comedian Tim Conway.

The nonsensical premise of the 18 spots that Sharpe eventually produced was virtually the same as the one he and Coyle had created: Sharpe and Anderson would set out to do a taste-test comparison between Bell Brand potato chips and an unnamed rival chip. Product-comparison commercials still carried with them a legacy of Brand X and the implicit understanding that no competitor would egregiously disparage another—it wasn't until campaigns such as the Pepsi Challenge in the 1980s that head-to-head comparisons became commonplace; in the sixties, Sharpe went out of his way not to discredit the other chip. Instead, he constructed situations where the utter silliness of the comparison was the root of the humor.

In all of the commercials Sharpe recorded along a stretch of Hollywood Boulevard, the central idea remained the same: Sharpe and Anderson would conduct bogus tests on Bell Brand potato chips, incorporating the "fresh, crisp and yummy" slogan and a reference to the chip inspector television campaign. Each commercial is as distinctive and unique as the real people Sharpe and Anderson commandeered on the street. In one spot, a French tourist is pressed into spontaneously translating the Bell Brand jingle into his native language. Another man is asked to fly across the Pacific in a balloon and drop Bell Brand chips over Japan. Sharpe and Anderson try to convince a reluctant renter to defy his mean-spirited landlady and decorate his apartment floor with Bell Brand potato chips. One taste test involved getting a man to eat Bell Brand chips with a candy mint and then dousing the rival chip in castor oil. There were silly magic tricks, chips stuffed into a corncob pipe, even chips rubbed with deodorant. In the final spot of the series, Anderson and Sharpe try to reminisce about the campaign with a hapless man on the street who hadn't heard any of the spots.

Some of the ads stand out more than others. In "Pickle," Sharpe and Anderson come upon a woman with a foreign accent and a little dog she calls Mishka. First referencing the Bell Brand chip inspector commercials, Sharpe directs Anderson to feed the dog a Bell Brand chip. Naturally, the dog eats it. Next, Anderson feeds the dog a chip that has been rejected by the inspector, but the dog won't eat it. But here's the gag— rather than a chip, Anderson is actually trying to feed the dog a pickle. Sharpe laughs, the woman laughs, and the singer in the tag sings the jingle, "If it's Bell—(*Ding!*)—it's swell!"

In another spot, "Test of Fire," Sharpe and Anderson have a man use a cigarette lighter to try to ignite a Bell Brand chip. The Bell Brand chip briefly catches fire then goes out. Sharpe then tries to light the rival chip. The hapless interview subject gets so involved with the little test that he posits that the test proves the Bell Brand is better quality. However, Anderson tells him the test proves absolutely nothing, and he has no idea what it means. "You got me," the fellow says contritely, "you got me in a way that I don't know the value of this to your company." The spot continues with Sharpe getting the guy to say the "fresh, crisp and yummy" slogan, which the man calls an odd description. "Aha, see," Anderson says, as if to provide conclusive proof of nothing in this Mad Hatter logic.

In another spot, "Shoe Polish," Sharpe offers a woman some dip to go along with her Bell Brand chips. Again, Sharpe recites the "fresh, crisp and yummy" slogan, only to find out that the woman always buys the rival chip. "Very good," she says after tasting the Bell Brand chip. Anderson then tries to get her to taste the rival chip with its dip—which happens to be shoe polish. Naturally, the woman refuses. Anderson and Sharpe press on, as they do in the other spots, to turn her reluctance into "proof" that Bell Brand potato chips are better, "as long as you don't eat it with shoe polish." It ends with the musical tag, as all the spots do, in a kind of symbolic wink that says it's all been in good fun.

Why do these spots still sound funny almost 40 years later? Certainly it's not the taste-test premise, which has since become trite. What makes Sharpe's twisted testimonials work is simply the people. Sharpe wasn't just on the street reciting copy points. As he says, "The spots were good because we got a really good person. You got the personality of the people into the spot."

The attraction of any testimonial is that the listener identifies with the commonness of the person being interviewed. The person in the testimonial becomes the symbolic customer. The humor is a product of that person being caught in Sharpe's disarmingly ingenuous interview. It's radio vérité, the same silliness that makes slapstick humor funny, only it's a verbal banana peel that the person slips on.

The listener believes that Sharpe's Bell Brand commercials happened exactly the way they sound on the radio. Copy points seem to flow effortlessly from strangers on the street. Regular folks willingly go along with Sharpe's preposterously bogus taste tests. Therein lies Sharpe's genius: What sounds like total spontaneity on tape is actually a carefully crafted commercial from beginning to end. "While I'm sort of known for the interviews," Sharpe says, "no one really realizes all the work in conceptualizing things that will work, and then not only editing but understanding what will make a story in 55 seconds—and still keep the flavor of the folks on the street."

Just as in any advertising project, the process begins with a conceptual premise. Before Sharpe hit the street, he would conceptualize "20 or 40 ideas" and then share them with the creative director of the advertising agency that had hired him for the assignment. Sharpe's premise list is like a quarterback's playbook, allowing him to capitalize on any opportunity. While doing one Bell Brand spot on Hollywood Boulevard, an entire troupe of Hare Krishna devotees danced by, chanting and making music with their bells and tambourines. Some quick thinking by Sharpe and Anderson had them offering up the ubiquitous "Hare Krishna, Hare Krishna" mantra as a new Bell Brand jingle. (Unfortunately, the leaders of the local Hare Krishna movement wanted too much money for their permission, and the Bell Brand client shelved the spot.)

Sharpe's success in capturing the copy points for the Bell Brand spot in a stream of reality consciousness isn't as easy as it sounds; the trick is in the editing. Sharpe spent hours editing the reels of quarter-inch audiotape on his trusty Uher recorder after he got home. But he was actually editing in his mind even as he was directing the street interview, much like a magician directs the unsuspecting subject of a trick to make the correct move. "Sometimes, I'd go back to the beginning of the interchange just to get a louder sentence. When people are warmed up a bit I ask them, 'What kind of work do you do?' And now they say it with authority." You can hear this technique in the "Pickle" commercial as Sharpe sets up the gag for the end line by asking the woman, "Why won't your poochie eat the rival chip?" "Because it's a pickle," she says, exactly as Sharpe planned.

Although the entertainment in Sharpe's interviews stems from the one-minute human interest stories, the commercials also act as advertising haikus to ensure that the client's time and money aren't being wasted on pure silliness. Sharpe repeats the product name often in the spots and makes sure he includes the copy points clearly and simply. The result is that the brand personality of Bell Brand potato chips comes across throughout the commercial as friendly, good-natured, fun, and snappy—what better qualities for a potato chip?

Sharpe has continued his advertising career and repeated his uniquely personal style for a host of products since the sixties. Over the past 40 years, he has used his affable and offbeat interviews to sell Ponctillos brand Minneapolis-based pizza to Italians in Rome, Italy; he has asked people in the Pacific Northwest what electricity smelled like for Pacific Power & Light; and he has pestered a recalcitrant Joe Montana on his Cellular One car phone to endorse the very product he was using.

Sharpe's style is uniquely his own, and commercials that attempt to copy it pale in comparison. However, radio copywriters can find lessons in Sharpe's sleight-of-mike techniques that can be applied to any good commercial:

1. Be flexible.

Whether you are working on the street, on location, or in the studio, be open to serendipity. Sharpe knew what he wanted when he went out on the street, but he had prepared other ideas in case opportunities presented themselves. Certainly it is incumbent on the copywriter and director to record the commercial as it was approved by the client. Make sure you cover the copy points. But if your original idea starts to head into a different, perhaps better, direction, go with it. When Sharpe encountered the Hare Krishna chanters on Hollywood Boulevard, he quickly incorporated their mantra into a potential jingle for Bell Brand. If you've covered the basics and have one "in the can," try something else. Perhaps having the actors switch roles would offer a new take. If the copy isn't flowing the way you thought it would when you wrote it, be flexible enough to try a quick rewrite in the studio, eliminating a line or two or rearranging how the copy tracks. Even improvisational actors in a recording studio, once they get over their need to act, says Sharpe, can help you discover an interesting spin on your first idea.

2. Say it straight.

Don't play hide-and-seek with the copy points. Make your points clear. This doesn't mean being boring or dull. But the sooner you can communicate the product, or the solution the product offers, the better your chance of a listener remembering what you're selling. "Some people go through such hoops that you don't know what the commercial is about," says Sharpe. Radio works best as a medium that can entertain and inform. It works even better when the entertainment serves to inform the audience about the product or service. Keep the message simple and work it into the concept of the spot. Remember that the radio audience isn't listening as hard as you or the client. So say it straight. Be up front about what you're selling.

3. Look for ideas everywhere.

When Sharpe was working as a radio copywriter for Chuck Blore, he often got a lot of ideas for commercials by looking at anything *but* the strategic copy brief for inspiration. "I was once looking at a picture of a camel crossing the desert and I wanted to get that feeling into a radio spot without two people talking about it." He used sound effects and music rather than dialogue. Sharpe also often diagrams the flow of his commercials, making a graphic representation of a disconnecting premise that would result in a humorous resolution. **Radio may be an audio medium, but it communicates through sound pictures; so thinking visually, looking at photos or artwork,**

imagining how the radio commercial might look in real life, can help you come up with an idea. Consider the product itself: Does it make any sounds, or are there sounds associated with it? What about the people who use the product? Are they unusual or inspiring? Sharpe found his ideas on the street for Bell Brand. "Radio is so great," says Mal Sharpe, "it really connects with people in a way that nothing else does."

Bell Brand Chips
"Pickle"
Used by permission of Man-On-The-Street Productions

MAL: Do you ever see the chip inspector on TV?

WOMAN: No, I don't get much chance to watch TV.

MAL: She inspects potato chips. And the bad ones she rejects. And the good ones she keeps for Bell Brand. Now I noticed you have a little poochie, a little dog with you.

WOMAN: Oh, he loves potato chips.

MAL: The dog loves potato chips? What's his name?

WOMAN: Mishka.

MAL: Now, what are you going to do, Mr. Anderson?

ANDERSON: I'm going to give the dog one of the Bell Brand potato chips that the inspector has passed to Mishka . . .

MAL: Let's see . . .

ANDERSON: And we'll see how he likes it.

MAL: Now Ernie is bending down, he's feeding the dog.

WOMAN: Mishka . . .

ANDERSON: Here we go Mishka . . .

SFX: Crunch.

MAL: What did the dog just do?

WOMAN: Finished off the potato chip.

ANDERSON: Now, this is a rejected chip. This chip was rejected by our Bell Brand inspector and I'm going to give it to Mishka, and you . . . you . . .

ANDERSON: [BG] Here, Mishka.

MAL: What's happening now?

WOMAN: [*Laughs*] He won't touch it.

MAL: What would you say is the reason why the rejected chip wasn't eaten by your little poochie?

WOMAN: The reason why he wouldn't eat the rejected potato chip was because it was a pickle.

[*Laughter*]

SINGER: If it's Bell [SFX: *Ding!*], it's swell.

Bell Brand
"Shoe Polish"
Used by permission of Man-On-The-Street Productions

MAL: First of all, we want you to try some Bell Brand potato chips. Have you ever had Bell Brand?

WOMAN: Ooooh yes . . .

MAL: Fresh, crisp and yummy, that's the word.

WOMAN: Oh.

MAL: Oh, you dipped it in the thing. How's it taste with the dip?

WOMAN: Very good.

MAL: How do you feel about the rival potato chip?

WOMAN: That's the one I purchase all the time.

ANDERSON: Well, I think this is going to work out just grand, Mal.

MAL: This is good, I think we're finally giving the rival chip an opportunity. Well let's see. Do we have some more dip?

ANDERSON: We have some nice dip for you for the rival chip.

WOMAN: I won't dip it in that though.

MAL: Why?

ANDERSON: We just want to see how good the rival chip goes with the dip.

WOMAN: No, not with that. I'm sorry. I wouldn't chance it with that.

MAL: Just dip it in there.

ANDERSON: [BG] Now would you put it in the dip, please?

WOMAN: That's shoe polish.

MAL: Oh, come on now, this is just . . .

WOMAN: That's shoe polish. I'm a good sport but . . . [*Laughs*] I'm not putting a potato chip in shoe polish!

MAL: Here on the street today, which tasted better, the Bell Brand with the dip or the rival chip?

WOMAN: Well, naturally, the Bell Brand with the dip.

MAL: And why did it go better?

WOMAN: Because it's a good chip, it's a good product.

MAL: As long as you don't eat it with shoe polish.

WOMAN: As long as you don't eat it with shoe polish, is right.

[*Laughter*]

SINGER: If it's Bell [SFX: *Ding!*], it's swell.

> Bell Brand
> "Chips on the Floor"
> Used by permission of Man-On-The-Street Productions

MAN: That's right, I'm a housepainter.

MAL: Uh, the Bell Brand potato chip inspector has what she considers a unique decorating idea. She believes that in decorating our homes, if we put potato chips on the floors that the houses would have a more natural feeling.

MAN: I never thought about putting them on the floor. I don't know how my landlady would approve of it. 'Cause I got a real fussy landlady.

MAL: Let us go now to your house.

MAN: No, I can't. Can't. The landlady would flip her lid. She'd throw me out on the street.

MAL: You'd tell her that the chips are fresh, crisp and yummy. That Bell Brand chips . . .

MAN: Oh, she's a . . . landladies are peculiar ducks. The only thing they love is money. I ain't never seen a land-lady in my life that liked anything but the long green cash.

MAL: Would you take some home with you now?

MAN: I'll dump these on the floor. I'll dump 'em right in here. In my stomach. Potato chips are here to stay.

SFX: [*Laughter*]

SINGER: If it's Bell [SFX: *Ding!*], it's swell.

Bell Brand
"Chanting"
Used by permission of Man-On-The-Street Productions

BACKGROUND: Hare Krishna chanting and bells.

MAL: Well, this is Mal Sharpe along with Ernie Anderson, and, of course, in the background you hear the people of California chanting for Bell Brand to defeat the rival chip.

ERNIE: You can hear them as they sing "Bell ba Brand . . . Bell ba Brand . . . Bell ba Brand" in the background.

MAL: Ma'am you're out here and you can hear these people—do you think this is going to be good for sales?

WOMAN: Well, it's the new thing, it's the new "in" thing.

ERNIE: Do you understand what they're chanting?

CHANTERS: Hare Krishna, Hare Krishna.

WOMAN: Well, it doesn't sound like potato chips at all.

MAL: What does it sound like?

WOMAN: It sounds like an Indian chant. . . . I mean, it's incongruous.

MAL: So, in summation, you think it's going to be a good year for Bell Brand potato chips as long as there's chanting?

WOMAN: I don't think so. I think it's going to be a good year for Bell Brand regardless of the chanting because their product is so good.

MAL: Fresh, crisp, and yummy.

WOMAN: Oh, very. Now what else do you want from me?

SINGER: If it's Bell [SFX: *Ding!*], it's swell.

Bell Brand
"Test of Fire"
Used by permission of Man-On-The-Street Productions

MAL: Both cigarette lighters work. Both you gentlemen now have potato chips.

MAN: Forgive me, this is all new to me. . . . Go ahead.

ERNIE: This is known as the Bell Brand test of fire.

MAN: I'm ready.

ERNIE: Now, would you light yours, please?

MAN: Yeah, all right.

MAL: What are you doing? You're lighting your potato . . .

MAN: I'm holding the potato chip over the flame.

MAL: Bell Brand potato chip, right? Now, Mr. Anderson, you're lighting the rival potato chip.

ERNIE: I'm now lighting the rival chip with my lighter.

MAL: Now, the Bell Brand thing was ignited briefly, right?

MAN: Yes it did. Just now it ignited briefly, but went right out. Now that is the test, gentlemen, meaning the quality would be better in the Bell Brand. Is that it?

MAL: No, it has nothing to do with quality.

ERNIE: We have no idea what that means.

MAN: You got me. You got me. You got me in a way that I don't know the value of this to your company.

ERNIE: Bell Brand potato chip inspector doesn't even know what that proves.

MAL: What do you think it proves?

MAN: I'd hate to hazard a guess on that one. . . .

MAL: Like the Bell Brand potato chip, was this test fresh, crisp, and yummy?

MAN: Very new and novel.

MAL: Not new and novel.

MAN: Fresh crisp . . . crisp and yummy. That's an odd description.

ERNIE: Aha! See!

SINGER: If it's Bell [SFX: *Ding!*], it's swell.

⑤ Blue Nun Wine: Stiller and Meara Give a Product a Personality

Client: Blue Nun Wine—Sichel, Schiefflein & Company

Agency: Della Femina, Travisano & Partners

Production Company: Stiller & Meara

Date: 1969–1982

In 1963, Julia Child capitalized on the budding interest in fine cuisine by introducing the art of fine French cooking to America on her PBS television program, *The French Chef*. Culinary standards were raised almost overnight and popularized across the country. Wine became more than a drink for culture snobs, immigrants, and lushes: It was touted as an integral part of a proper dining experience. Suddenly, a dinner in a fancy restaurant became a terrifying experience for millions of nouveau gourmets who faced the challenge of ordering the correct wine—red or white? The right answer, according to a creative collaboration between an advertising wunderkind and an unlikely married comedy team was simple: Order Blue Nun wine.

One of the most memorable and effective radio campaigns in advertising history, Blue Nun radio commercials started their 13-year run in 1969 when they were created by Jerry Stiller and Anne Meara for the New York advertising agency, Della Femina, Travisano & Partners. The classic repartee between the seasoned comedy team turned a $3 bottle of German liebfraumilch wine into a cultural icon. Not only was Blue Nun the correct wine for any dish (as the tag line put it, "going as well with meat as it did with fish"), but it was also the subject of a campaign that paired the approachable, down-to-earth comedy of Stiller and Meara with the provocative marketing genius of Jerry Della Femina. The commercials racked up spectacular sales for the imported wine over the life of the campaign. More than 30 years later, the commercials still demonstrate the value of finding the right talent, the benefit of building an audio brand identity, and the art of making a perfect marriage between concept and product.

According to Stiller's autobiography, *Married to Laughter*, Della Femina cast the comedy team years after first seeing them in a New York Greenwich Village nightclub called Phase II. In the sixties, Stiller and Meara's two-person humor was very popular in nightclubs, on comedy records, and on the radio. Comedy duos had been around since Laurel and Hardy, Abbott and Costello, Bob Hope and Bing Crosby, Jerry Lewis and Dean Martin, and they'd been on radio with George Burns and Gracie Allen. In the 1960s, the tradition continued with a radical twist true to the times, as Mike Nichols and Elaine May brought their martini-dry style of comedy to nightclubs in Greenwich Village, and Jack Burns and Avery Schreiber featured the improvisational repartee of the Second City comedy troupe in their act. And, as ethnic humor began to enter the popular entertainment arena, Jerry Stiller and Anne Meara got tremendous laugh mileage from their Jewish-Irish marriage of opposites. As a March 1975 *Newsweek* article put it, "The stubby, pensive Stiller and the tall, zanily ebullient Meara . . . go together about as well as ham on a bagel."

The use of the duo's sketches to pitch a sweet, inexpensive imported German wine was as much the brainchild of Della Femina, an enfant terrible of the advertising world, as it was a product of the highly creative period of countercultural advertising in the late 1960s and early 1970s. As Lawrence Dobson said in his history of the time, *When Advertising Tried Harder: The Sixties: The Golden Age of American Advertising*, it was a period of intense creativity. Doyle Dane Bernbach revolutionized the style, look, and feel of advertising. Its Volkswagen print ads and the Alka-Seltzer "Spicy Meatball" TV commercial and campaign for Avis Rent A Car advanced the state of advertising. Much of the humor in advertising from that period reflected the influx of Jewish and Italian writers and art directors, such as Della Femina, who stepped on the white-shoe propriety of old-line, traditional, Madison Avenue shops. Many, like Della Femina, left advertising agencies like Ted Bates & Company to start their own firms, trading on their brand of more ethnic, hipper, contemporary advertising. *Advertising Age* later named Della Femina one of the 100 most influential advertising people of the century, a distinction based on his early work such as his concept for using Stiller and Meara to sell Blue Nun.

Stiller recounted in his autobiography how the Blue Nun commercials were born. The upstart agency Della Femina, Travisano & Partners had won the Blue Nun wine account from importer Schiefflein & Company just two years after the agency was founded in 1967. Della Femina needed a creative solution for what was usually thought of as a marketing nightmare: how to sell a sweet, simple, fruity German wine to an unsophisticated audience. True to his role as advertising agency provocateur, Della Femina figured he would take the stuffiness and mystique out of an imported product like Blue Nun. And who better to do that than the Everyman and Everywoman of Stiller and Meara? Unlike the cerebral, intellectual characters portrayed by Nichols and May, Stiller and Meara had strong ethnic New York accents that made them "just plain folks." The average Irish and Jewish and often Italian characters that populated Stiller and Meara's comedy routines mirrored the kind of people who were the audience for Blue Nun wine. Aiming for these regular people was a particularly good choice considering that the average diner was then intimidated about ordering the right wine to accompany a meal.

As Stiller recounts, Della Femina invited them up to his office to improvise a commercial on the spot into a tape recorder. Meara began by making up a scenario on how the wine got its name—a story about the teetotaling, grape-crushing nuns who were "blue" because they never got to taste of the fruits of their labor. Meara had them drink the wine and get sick. The shtick cracked Della Femina up. Of course, the real story for the product's name came from two actual German nuns who tirelessly tried to promote German products after World War II. At first they wore their traditional brown habits, but when one gave up the mission, the other changed into a friendlier blue habit.

Back in his office, Della Femina did a setup for Stiller and Meara to improvise a couple on a date in a restaurant with the young man trying to impress his date. They can't decide on the wine, and Della Femina as the waiter suggests a little Blue Nun. Meara replies, "Wasn't she on the *Ed Sullivan Show?*" She was referring jokingly to the then-popular guitar-playing singing nun. The ad man broke up and offered the comedy team the job of creating the campaign right then and there (p. 230). It was just the type of character humor he was looking for, and from that moment on, Stiller and Meara created radio commercials that played on the "absently present" Blue Nun character.

In all, Stiller and Meara worked with Della Femina to create 33 commercials over the 13-year campaign. More often than not, the characters portrayed by Stiller and Meara were in a bar, a restaurant, a liquor store, a disco—anywhere it was logical for two people to be discussing wine. In one commercial, Stiller is on the prowl at a singles resort. He suggests a luncheon beverage to his addlepated pickup, offering her a little Blue Nun; Meara as the floozy asks if she is the "one in the little black pedal pushers."

Often, the premise of a spot was based on the confusion surrounding the name, Blue Nun. Building the joke around the repetition of the Blue Nun name in the commercial not only made for good, memorable advertising, but also helped establish the brand name as a brand *character* beyond the bottle's label, much like other fictional popular advertising characters such as Uncle Ben, Betty Crocker, and Tony the Tiger. Whether the Blue Nun was mistaken for the popular 1960s Belgian "Singing Nun," Dominican Sister Sourire Luc Gabrielle or a patron in the innumerable bars and restaurants where the commercials were set or eventually just the name of the wine, Stiller and Meara established a strong visual image. In fact, Della Femina described an atypical approach for creating the Blue Nun commercials: Similarly to a television spot, each commercial was drawn as a storyboard, a series of scenes to ensure a strong visual feel to the radio script.

In another commercial, Meara is consoling herself alone at dinner after being dumped by her boyfriend, Carmine Manicotti. When Stiller, who is playing the waiter, asks what she wants, she answers "Manicotti." He assumes she is ordering the Italian stuffed pasta dish; Meara corrects him that it's her former boyfriend, and the spot is off with a round of mistaken identity, including the requisite Blue Nun confusion. It ends with Stiller suggesting to Meara some "cantaloupe" for after dinner. She doesn't see it on the menu, and now it's his turn to clarify that his name is Stanley Cantelope, the guy, not the fruit, and he wants to take her out after he gets off work. It's the same kind of almost vaudevillian humor made famous by Abbott and Costello in their linguistic ping-pong game of "Who's On First?"

To keep a long-running campaign fresh, many writers draw on topical issues of the day. In one Blue Nun commercial that embodies many of the cultural trends of the early seventies, Stiller is shopping in a liquor store for a bottle of red wine to celebrate his wedding anniversary while his wife is home cooking his favorite dinner, liver and onions. Meara plays a liberated, braless wine salesperson who dresses Stiller down for making his wife "cry her eyes out over onions." She then gushes over her feminist husband Wendell, who even "picks up the kids from nursery, makes a delicious bouillabaisse, and still manages to look gorgeous." Meara says she and Wendell are also celebrating the anniversary of her burning her bra. In a great one-liner, Stiller says he noticed, and Meara replies simply, "Suffer." The spot plays off the male-female role reversals that went on during the early seventies. Stiller's final comments that Wendell's domestic role is his way of "dodging the draft" are the kicker that sets the spot solidly in its time. It's all captured with the perfectly timed, soft-selling comedic banter that made Stiller and Meara famous.

Although the final recorded spots sound as smooth and practiced as a well-oiled vaudeville routine, Stiller recalled how one of the spots wasn't that easy to do. One commercial that Della Femina directed required 30 takes—quite a high number considering the professionalism of the talent. Years later, Stiller asked Della Femina about it and the ad man replied that the couple had actually nailed the commercial recording on the first take, but he wanted to let them try to make it even better.

With only Stiller and Meara's voices carrying almost all of the commercials, there is a kind of purity to the spots—devoid of sound effects, music, or background ambience. Stiller and Meara's brand of humor, honed in the days of Greenwich Village boîtes, was always about their voices, their words, and their interactions. Their personalities carried the brand and built such strong associations with it that it increased their popularity. When the couple was seen around New York city locations—in restaurants and shops—people would ask them if they really drink the wine. "We bathe in it," Meara would snap back.

A good part of the success for the Blue Nun sales can be attributed not only to Stiller and Meara, but also to the willingness of Schiefflein & Company to invest in a healthy media plan. With national distribution of the wine, it was necessary to have a national media buy. Though in the early seventies network television dominated most national buys as network radio virtually disappeared, the Della Femina, Travisano media planners crafted a media plan that, by 1975, put the Blue Nun commercials on the air in 275 U.S. cities. Four years later, the campaign was airing in 40 markets (each one representing a large number of individual cities) with a light media buy of network radio.

In spite of Stiller and Meara's success, even in the late sixties and early seventies, there was still a lingering doubt over the effectiveness of humor in advertising. Articles in both *Advertising Age* and the *Wall Street Journal* at the time trotted out the tired objections to using laughter to sell. Once again, the naysayers were wrong. The well-crafted Blue Nun commercials made humor an integral part of the sell. Della Femina proved that a few chuckles from a listener could translate to more than a few shekels at the cash register.

In addition, *Advertising Age* rated the Blue Nun campaign among the top 100 of the century. The campaign won numerous advertising awards, most notably a Clio in 1975 for its creativity and an Effie in 1978 for its effectiveness. And effective it was. Every year the Stiller and Meara commercials ran, sales of Blue Nun increased. In 1969, Schiefflein & Company was selling around 60,000 cases a year on an ad budget of about $200,000. Ten years later, the ad budget had grown to $4 million, and case sales were up to 1.2 million. By 1976, Blue Nun had become America's best-selling imported white wine.

The Della Femina campaign finished its run in 1980 when the venerable *New York Times* ad columnist Phil Dougherty reported that J. Penn Kavanagh, the same man who had approved the campaign years earlier as a young assistant ad manager and who later became president of Schiefflein, put the account up for review, ultimately awarding it to the Cunningham & Walsh agency in May 1980. Though the Della Femina Stiller and Meara campaign had pushed the sales to 60 percent annual gains early on, the final years were not as profitable. Looking to move the campaign to television to reach a larger audience of more sophisticated consumers, Kavanagh had the new agency cast a New York actress, Cathy O'Reilly, to play the

Blue Nun in a series of TV commercials. But it is Stiller and Meara people will always associate with Blue Nun.

Copywriters, clients, and producers can learn plenty from the Blue Nun campaign:

1. Find the right talent.

The right voice-over talent can make or break a commercial. Many young actors get their start in radio, and many seasoned pros with highly recognizable voices find advertising a lucrative gig. Besides listening to voices on the demo reels that casting and talent agents send out to promote their clients, try cultivating other places to find talent for your commercial to make it stand out and be memorable. Della Femina discovered Stiller and Meara in a small Greenwich Village nightclub years before he thought to cast them in the Blue Nun commercials. Go to comedy clubs where new comedians are getting started to find people who have the quick wit, improvisational technique, or unusual voices to make your commercial stand out. Local theater productions are another venue for potential voice-over talent that hasn't been heard on the air before. Tune in to Saturday morning cartoon shows—many voice-over actors make a good living doing the voices behind the animated characters—and watch the credits to see who did the voice that caught your attention. If you're daring and the script for the commercial is appropriate, you can even cast nonprofessional voices. It requires more work, but you can get a very natural sound, and you just might discover a diamond in the rough.

2. Establish an audio brand identity.

Just as a successful and effective product brand identity is created by carefully managing the graphic elements, the logo, and colors and packaging, it is important to establish a powerful audio brand identity through parallel audio elements. Stiller and Meara built the brand identity for Blue Nun, and in return the popular commercials established a reputation for Stiller and Meara. Their highly recognizable voices, the predictable patter, and consistent mnemonic product message embodied in the tag line ("the delicious wine that goes as well with meat as it does with fish") helped to establish an audio brand identity for Blue Nun. There are other ways to build brand on the radio. A recurring musical tag on the end of the commercials is commonly used. Using the same announcer with a highly recognizable voice is a very easy way to maintain continuity and consistency over a long-running campaign. Even a thematic approach—in which the subject matter links the product with execution—can help build the brand. One award-winning, long-running campaign that aired on a classical music station linked an insurance company's expertise for covering valuable personal property, such as jewelry and artwork, with references to jewelry and precious objects in classical music and opera. **Repetition, consistency, and familiarity will lead to recognition for a product's audio brand.**

3. Marry your concept to your product.

Della Femina chose Stiller and Meara to introduce and promote Blue Nun because the couple embodied the typical middle American audience that Schiefflein importers were trying to target. The situations that Stiller and Meara created in their commercials—the waiter and diner, wine shopper and sales clerk, bar hopper and floozy, and others—provided a realistic and believable venue to promote the product. The concept supported the benefits and uses of the product. Too often, radio commercials disconnect the humorous, entertaining part of the pitch with the informational sales message. When working through the various ideas before scripting a commercial, develop those concepts that put the product in an appropriate and relevant context. For instance, if the product is an ice tea mix, consider all the possibilities where it would be used—on a beach in the summer, on a camping trip, at a party, by kids. A vacuum cleaner commercial might give humorous voice to the dirt particles being sucked up. **Make humor the offspring of a marriage between product and concept.**

⑥ *Time* Magazine: Dick and Bert Showcase Fanatical Devotion

Client: *Time* Magazine
Agency: Young & Rubicam
Production Company: Dick & Bert
Date: 1977–1980

From its first issue on March 3, 1923, *Time* magazine has chronicled the history of modern times. The magazine that Henry Luce and Briton Hadden invented has been true to its vision of being a lookout for news and trends for the past 79 years. So it is only fitting that the radio commercials created by Dick Orkin and Bert Berdis for *Time* magazine in the late 1970s should also figure prominently in the history of radio advertising. Their unique approach to comedy in the service of delivering a commercial message altered forever the course of humorous radio ads, opening up innovative avenues of creative expression and inviting whole new categories of advertisers to radio.

Over a period of three years, from 1977 to 1980, Dick and Bert wrote, produced, and acted in close to 30 commercials for *Time* magazine. The groundbreaking spots they created for *Time* under the aegis of the advertising agency Young & Rubicam aired in major markets—Los Angeles, New York, Chicago, and San Francisco. Described in a 1980 *Newsweek* article as "lunatic humor with a stirring sales pitch," Dick and Bert's *Time* magazine commercials "brilliantly evoke the *Angst* of modern man with his elemental dread of being *cut off from his magazines.*"

The commercials are a brilliant study in voice-acting per-formance, improvisational-style writing, witty humor, and sophisticated advertising salesmanship. And they were also the spark that ignited the business partnership of Dick & Bert. Though their particular brand of absurdist advertising humor might seem an unlikely fit with the conservatism of *Time,* the contradiction actually won people's attention. Dick and Bert's extraordinary teamwork, fresh inventiveness, and ability to cre-ate "real" characters in absurd situations are hallmarks of their genius.

By the late seventies, *Time* was considered the preeminent newsweekly magazine. It was the media buyer's vehicle of choice for reaching an educated, intelligent, and mainstream audience. It was an audience *Time* had planned to reach from its inception. In a review of a lecture on Henry Luce delivered by Professor Alan Brinkley, noted history scholar, Jason Hol-lander explained in the *Columbia News* that the journalistic suc-cess of *Time* was due in part to the "more sophisticated and culturally aware" middle class "which emerged in great num-bers during the boom years after World War I." Luce saw *Time,* according to Professor Brinkley, as a publication "that would interpret the news for those who could not do so on their own." In a special 75th anniversary issue that is a paean to its founder, *Time* reported that Luce wanted the magazine to be a "point of connection between the world of elite ideas and opinion and middle-class people . . . hungry for knowledge." It was a natu-ral fit, then, for media buyers to place ads in *Time* that appealed to this audience—ads for serious automobiles such as Cadillacs, conservative banks and financial institutions, and upscale lux-ury goods.

That was all well and good for the "front of the book," as the serious news section in the forward pages of the magazine is called. But magazines are on a constant quest to increase the number of advertising pages—a fat book is a financially healthy book. And so the job of reaching new advertisers for the "back of the book"—the sections devoted to art, music, theater, dance, and cinema—went to *Time*'s advertising agency in 1977, Young & Rubicam. One of the longtime stalwarts of Madison Avenue, Y&R had long been known for its expertise in radio advertising. In fact, it was Y&R that used another comedy team, Bob Elliott and Ray Goulding, to bring its brand of humor to radio commercials in the early fifties, with characters Bert and Harry Piel for the Brooklyn-based brand, Piels beer. In the seventies, Y&R was also the ad agency for another Time Inc. publication, *People,* which was a mere three years old in 1977. It was this connection between *People* and *Time* that actually first brought Dick Orkin and Bert Berdis along their path to advertising history.

The early successes of Dick and Bert's first radio spots caught the attention of Y&R creative director, Jerry Smith, who asked them to bid on a package for radio commercials for *People* magazine. Charles Nelson Reilly and Dick Cavett were also asked to do demo commercials. Although the Reilly/Cavett spots were chosen initially over the demos that Dick and Bert submitted, three months later Y&R came back and asked Orkin and Berdis to pitch *Time* with a campaign similar to the one they had proposed for *People.*

The actual objective of the *Time* campaign was to woo media buyers into recommending *Time*'s more youthful, culturally focused back-of-the-book sections for their younger, hipper advertisers, such as purveyors of sports cars, soft drinks, and popular fashion brands. Orkin recalls that *Time* "wasn't getting motorcycles and the newer model cars . . . and so they wanted to find a way of reaching the media buyers with the message that *Time* is not as old fogy and stodgy as you think it is."

How they met that objective was realized in the series of 60-second performance pieces created by Dick and Bert. Their personal histories as actors, stand-up comics, and storytellers were important ingredients in shaping a style of commercial that had never been heard before. True, Bob Elliott and Ray

Goulding had invented silly characters for their radio spoofs and occasional commercial ventures, and Stan Freberg used his offbeat humor and production genius to create complex commercials that were breakthrough in their own right, but no one had ever before used all the essential elements of theater and storytelling—conflict, character, setting, and dialogue—quite like Dick and Bert.

Orkin's serious training at the Yale drama school and Berdis's comic career as a sketch writer for Jackie Gleason and as an improv actor with *Second City* contributed to the farcical *Time* spots. As Berdis described the commercials, they're "like little plays . . . with a beginning, there's a middle, and there's an end. Hopefully there's a denouement. And then there are little tangents you can take off on . . . every spot we ever did there's a conflict. . . . It's all character driven . . . and they're all acting pieces."

In the spot titled, "Ripper," two patients in a doctor's waiting room fight over a *Time* magazine as one fellow insists on ripping out the pages. In "Banana Boat," a *Time*-absorbed toll-bridge operator is being fired by his boss, the Commissioner of Bridges and Sidewalks, for failing to raise a bridge for a banana boat's arrival in Herndon, Iowa. Two airline passengers argue over who gets the *Time* magazine first. A suburbanite dressed in his wife's frilly housecoat with puffy sleeves is picked up by the cops while on a late-night foray to get a *Time* before going to bed. Each of these commercials, and all the others in the campaign, has a conflict surrounding the magazine that creates an opportunity to highlight the features, stories, sections, and coverage in a natural, albeit absurd, story line.

True to good theatrical writing, the *Time* commercials are always set in a specific locale—a train station, a river toll bridge, the showroom of an imported-car dealership, an airplane, or the bedroom of a newsdealer at 3 A.M. That kind of exacting auditory-induced visual imagery helped make the commercials all the more memorable.

That radio is a theater of the mind is trite but evident in the silly situations Dick and Bert established with a minimum of sound effects. The spots, in the end, are really finely honed miniature "dramadies" in which the acting carries the weight of the commercial's sales job. As Orkin recalled, "Both of us had acting backgrounds, especially improv backgrounds, so we used that . . . in fact, most observers of advertising were pretty much convinced that we had ad-libbed those spots, when in fact we didn't. We never did. We just had the capacity to read them in a way that made them sound like they were improvised in the moment."

Not unlike the early club work of Jerry Stiller and Anne Meara and Mike Nichols and Elaine May (who were early role models for Berdis), the commercials that Dick and Bert created sounded improvised but were carefully scripted. Orkin recalled, "Occasionally, we'd take some liberty with a line instead of using the line as scripted . . . but we rarely broke away from the copy." But even the writing has a simplicity to it that allows each actor to make the most of a character's vocal tics and quirks, all the while setting up the joke. The writing process involved Dick and Bert sitting at a dining-room table, trading lines while writing, working out the give-and-take rhythm of the scenario before they ever got into a recording studio.

Perhaps the only line that Dick and Bert didn't write for the spots was the tag line, "*Time* makes everything more interesting. Including you." This was written by a copywriter at Y&R and performed by Jim Coyne, an ad agency employee who happened to have a passable announcer's voice. When Dick and Bert were doing the demos, "he did it and *Time* liked it and it was like a windfall for him," remembers Berdis. Later, the tag line was changed to, "*Time,* the most colorful coverage of the week," in order to highlight the photography and more interesting writing style in the magazine.

What is essential to the commercials is the actors' performance. There are no jokes in any of the scripts; it is the delivery, the timing, the straight-man/dumb-guy setup that makes the commercials work. The humor is integral to the conceptual story line, not a rim-shot, one-shot gag. Drawing on his drama school training, Orkin knew that playing to the emotional truth of the moment—a tenet of improvisational and naturalistic acting—would contribute to humor. The characters in the *Time* spots are completely involved in their desire to read, acquire, borrow, or steal the magazine. The resulting confusion and conflict propels the spots forward. No matter how ludicrous, the characters are completely serious about their situation, and their seriousness contributes even more to the humor. By always giving their characters unique and distinctive qualities through the writing and their voices, Dick and Bert were able to draw listeners into the absurdity of the conflict in which the product—*Time* magazine—was always the hero.

Distinctively setting the commercials apart were the voices of Dick and Bert. Although they did occasionally hire voice-over actors (Annie Ryerson, Miriam Flynn, and others) when a script called for it, the first crop of spots featured Dick's neurotic, pathetic loser to Bert's unflappable straight man. Orkin said, "If I took away all the years of trained announcer voice when I was a DJ and got down to the basic character, the real self, there was gold in that . . . the truthfulness about the character made it far more fun for us than trying to do cartoony voices or caricature voices." In "Puffy Sleeves," Orkin's housecoated nerd stammers and whimpers nervously to the police officer, "Oh please, don't send me up the river just for wearing puffy sleeves." Again in "Banana Boat," Orkin's bridge operator tries to pass off a lame excuse to his boss, the Commissioner of Bridges and Sidewalks, that he was "reading a magazine" and therefore didn't hear the boat's whistle. Berdis's commissioner takes a microsecond of a silent beat, the auditory equivalent of a comedic slow burn, and redoubles his formal dismissal speech.

Dick and Bert also played the characters in their spots as being worse off than the audience rather than as the traditional role models customarily used in advertising. Embarrassed, ridiculous, and nervous characters populate the *Time* spots, complete with flaws like stutters and stammers. At the dramatic climax of their commercials, many of the characters are left dumbstruck and speechless, creating moments of dead air. For instance, when the haplessly dim car buyer finally understands that the *Time* magazine on the car seat is free only when you buy the $89,000 Fuchi Manuli sports car, he gulps, stammers, and runs from the showroom. No one had ever allowed their characters to speak as naturalistically and "unprofessionally," but Dick and Bert used this device to great comic effect.

Whether stopped by the police while wearing a puffy-sleeved housecoat late at night, misunderstanding a car dealer's gift of a *Time* magazine in an expensive car, or confronting an aggressive magazine page ripper in a doctor's waiting room, the characters fully embrace their absurdities. Dick and Bert knew that their level of humor made their ads distinctive. "We thought we were writing for sophisticated *Time* magazine media buyers," Orkin said. "So we . . . got a little bit more literary in our approach to it."

Humor in advertising had until then only been seen as appropriate for younger, more "fun" clients. In the *Time* magazine spots, humor is integral to the commercials, not additive, and the humor emerges from the absurd situations themselves instead of from jokes and gags. For example, when a high-society lady bids a tearful farewell to her upper-crust beau at the train station (in a homage to every movie train station farewell), she suddenly loses her society accent when she realizes he has stolen her *Time* magazine. When Orkin and Berdis play two airline passengers arguing over who gets to read *Time* magazine first, the humor is in Orkin's insistence that he be allowed to finish writing a letter to his "mommy" before surrendering the magazine to Berdis.

The outstanding critical, professional, and business success of the commercials paved the way for the use of humor for entirely new categories of advertisers. Suddenly, big banks, serious insurance companies, and prestigious automakers all vied for Dick and Bert's time and talent. After the first batch of commercials aired, *Time* decided to expand the target audience beyond the original media-space buyers and reach out to the general public as part of a campaign to increase newsstand sales. Once the campaign was rolling, Dick and Bert began working directly with *Time*'s publisher, Ralph Davidson, and only as a matter of courtesy did they show the scripts to Y&R for the ad agency's blessing. The relationship between *Time* and Dick and Bert was so cordial, in fact, that the *Time* promotional department used the pair as attractions for advertisers at sales junkets and "pours," those business social gatherings for big-ticket advertisers. Later, *Time* issued a compilation record album of the commercials. Many of the edgier concepts that Dick and Bert proposed for *Time* were rejected by the agency but applauded and approved by the magazine publisher. One such spot featured a man looking in a porno bookstore for *Time* because the shop featured "special magazines" and *Time* was special. The spot ran for a week or so, recalls Orkin, but then the agency suggested it be pulled to preserve *Time*'s pristine image.

But none of the commercials would have been produced if Dick and Bert had never formed their legendary duo in 1973. What really brought Berdis and Orkin together was simple economics. Berdis didn't want to stay at his Detroit ad agency job, so he pitched the idea to Orkin about starting their own commercial production company. Orkin asked Berdis for help in writing episodes of his radio serial, *Chicken Man,* and offered in return to help Berdis write commercials. Soon both realized that there was more money to be made in creating original radio commercials than in writing radio serials, and the firm of Dick & Bert was formed. Together, they began hitting advertising agencies in New York, Chicago, and Los Angeles, presenting themselves to creative directors as a small production house, literally, using as a prop a little cardboard house that Dick Orkin would wear on his head during the pitch.

Unlike the absurd characters whose idiosyncrasies spark the humor in their commercials, Dick and Bert's history-making, award-winning *Time* magazine radio spots were characterized by level-headed thinking, professional expertise, and careful craftsmanship that provides many lessons for copywriters, actors, and radio producers. In fact, Orkin has leveraged his academic background and formalized his approach for comedy radio writing into a series of lectures and seminars. He established his Radio Ranch in Hollywood, California, where to this day he continues to produce commercials. Across town in Los Angeles, Bert Berdis & Company is one of the leading commercial production companies in Hollywood, with recent forays into producing funny animation and voice-overs for business-to-business web sites.

Though Dick and Bert ended their partnership in the early eighties, their contribution to the art of radio advertising remains as fresh and current as ever.

1. Don't be obvious.

After digesting the strategy brief, consider the most obvious solutions. It's often easy to figure out trite ideas that create an opportunity for characters to talk about something: a game show, a psychiatric visit, a radio call-in talk show, a phone call. Even though these devices can work, they are ideas that have been done to death. **Try to find a strong concept that grows out of the product or service itself. Dick and Bert found ideas in people's fanatical devotion to *Time*, whether being engrossed in the magazine's stories, ripping out pages, stealing someone else's copy, or searching for an issue at all hours.** Explore ideas until you've come up with something that is new, or at least new to the category.

According to Bert Berdis, "if you have a really strong concept, anyone can write it."

2. Don't do it alone.

"Most agency writers sit alone in their cubicles and try and be as funny as the disc jockey they heard that morning. And that's wrong," Berdis says. **A huge element behind the success of Dick and Bert's commercials is the interplay between the characters. If you want to write two-part comedy spots, find a writing partner who shares your sensibilities. Look for someone who isn't afraid of conflict.** If you're going to start a fire, you need a few sparks. You can also find ideas for conflicts within the product or service itself. If you want to feature late hours or friendly service, create a conflict around a person who doesn't like late hours or friendly service. Don't just lay out the features—make them the crux of the conflict. And remember, it takes two people to give birth to a great idea.

3. Create a scene.

It's not really interesting to have two people just sitting around a breakfast table. "Put them in a dirigible over the Himalayas," Berdis says. With radio, you have to create a visual scene in the mind's eye. The more memorable the visual, the more memorable the spot. You can put your characters anywhere and move them around. You can transport a man wearing his wife's housecoat in a police car or set two upper-crust characters in a smoke-filled train station. Sound effects can help—a single cardoor slam is the only effect Dick and Bert use in the "Fuchi Manuli" spot. But radio can also be very effective using words alone to create a scene; you can almost see the 40-ton banana boat from Guatemala waiting at the drawbridge in Herndon, Iowa, even though we never hear a single toot. **Help your listeners picture where the action is taking place and you'll bring to scene to life.**

4. Cast your characters in your mind first.

Berdis and Orkin agree that by writing with a specific actor in mind, you're much more likely to write in a voice that will work. Even if that person cannot be hired to do the spot, it will help bring your character to life. For Dick and Bert, a guy who rips out magazine pages, a businessman who writes his mommy, a man in his housecoat, and a smarmy foreign-car salesman are all "real" people with their own personalities; the audience can imagine them living before and after the interlude of the commercial. **To create a character, start by imagining a person you might know, such as a relative, a friend, or a coworker, even just someone you overheard in the grocery store. Think about how that person would act in the situation you've created; then listen in your mind to how he or she might sound before you begin writing copy that doesn't sound like anyone at all. Once you've imagined a living, breathing character rather than a mouthpiece for the sponsor's messages, you'll find the words that would really come out of his or her mouth.**

Time Magazine
"Banana Boat"
Used by permission of Dick Orkin and Bert Berdis

COMMISSIONER: All you had to do was pull the switch and raise the bridge

BRIDGE OPERATOR: I know that, Commissioner.

COMMISSIONER: You were trained to raise bridges.

BRIDGE OPERATOR: I said I'm sorry.

COMMISSIONER: Well, as Commissioner of Bridges and Sidewalks, it is my duty to . . .

BRIDGE OPERATOR: There was a reason, you know.

COMMISSIONER: What?

BRIDGE OPERATOR: I was reading a magazine.

[*Pause*]

COMMISSIONER: It is my duty . . .

BRIDGE OPERATOR: Not just any magazine, a *Time* magazine . . . you know you just don't look up when you're reading *Time* magazine. . . .

COMMISSIONER: You do if it's a 40-ton banana boat from Guatemala . . .

BRIDGE OPERATOR: I didn't see it.

COMMISSIONER: . . . when it's sitting and tooting in front of a bridge for an hour and a half.

BRIDGE OPERATOR: Sir, you get caught up in a *Time* magazine. What are your interests? Theater? Art? Music? Books? Cinema? It's all there in *Time* magazine . . .

COMMISSIONER: It's taxidermy.

BRIDGE OPERATOR: Ow . . . well *Time* has a lot more color photography. Maybe there's a picture of something being st-st-stuffed. Let's take a look here.

SFX: [*Flipping pages*]

COMMISSIONER: It is my duty . . .

BRIDGE OPERATOR: Sir, it was a *Time* magazine. It's not like I was caught with my hands down in my pants in the till.

COMMISSIONER: Good grief, man. The boat had to turn around and go all the way back to Guatemala.

BRIDGE OPERATOR: You know, I've had a perfect record for 11 years here.

COMMISSIONER: We haven't had a boat here in Herndon, Iowa, for 11 years.

BRIDGE OPERATOR: Well that's being picky.

COMMISSIONER: It is my duty to inform you . . .

BRIDGE OPERATOR: One lousy mistake and you're making a big thing out of it.

ANNCR: *Time* makes everything more interesting. Including you.

Time Magazine
"Puffy Sleeves"
Used by permission of Dick Orkin and Bert Berdis

SFX: [*Car comes to stop*]

POLICEMAN: Pardon me, sir, would you step over here to the patrol car, please?

MAN: Oh..hel..hello, Officer.

POLICEMAN: Do you have business in this neighborhood, sir?

MAN: Yes. I live f-f-four blocks from here. It's the brick colonial with the crack in the driveway.

POLICEMAN: Um-hm. What are you doing out this time of night, sir?

MAN: Well, I got all ready for bed, see, and darned if I didn't forget to pick up a copy of *Time* magazine at the newsstand today.

POLICEMAN: What type of coat would you call that, sir?

MAN: Th-this is a h-h-housecoat. See, I spilled cocoa on mine and I just grabbed my wife's. I guess the puffy sleeves look a little silly. Ha ha . . .

SFX: [*Door opens*]

POLICEMAN: Do you want to get in the car, sir?

SFX: [*Door closes*]

SFX: [*Engine driving*]

MAN: In the car? See I just don't go to bed without a *Time* movie review or something from the Modern Living section.

POLICEMAN: Yes sir.

MAN: I tried reading something else, but there isn't anything like *Time*.

POLICEMAN: No.

MAN: Do you know, Officer, how many editorial awards *Time* magazine has won?

POLICEMAN: No sir, I don't.

MAN: And *Time* is so respected. And I'm a firm believer along with Winston Churchill that you are what you read.

POLICEMAN: Um-hm.

MAN: Oh, please, don't send me up the river just for wearing puffy sleeves.

POLICEMAN: You're home, sir.

MAN: I love . . . oh, thank . . . God bless . . . ahem . . . okay . . . bye.

SFX: [*Car door slam*]

ANNCR: *Time.* The most colorful coverage of the week.

Time Magazine
"Fuchi Manuli"
Used by permission of Dick Orkin and Bert Berdis

SALESMAN: Sir, the Fuchi Manuli is the finest automobile in the world.

MAN: Oh, I know that. It's just, $89,000 is more money than I had in mind.

SFX: [*Car door opens*]

SALESMAN: Look on the seat here. What do you see?

MAN: A magazine.

SALESMAN: This is not just a magazine, sir. This is the Fuchi Manuli of magazines. A *Time* magazine.

MAN: Oh, right. Someone leave it on the seat here?

SALESMAN: We left it on the seat for you.

MAN: Oh! I love *Time*. Great.

SALESMAN: It's our way of saying here is expert craftsmanship.

MAN: Yes.

SALESMAN: Here is an experience that's fast-moving and bright.

MAN: Right. Bright.

SALESMAN: Just like the Fuchi Manuli.

MAN: Yes.

SALESMAN: So why don't you go ahead and take it?

MAN: Thank you. I love this *Time* magazine.

SALESMAN: Good. Now what about delivery?

MAN: I'll just stick it in my briefcase. I don't need to . . .

SALESMAN: I meant the car.

MAN: Oh. Ha ha. You mean I have to take the $89 . . . to get the . . . I see.

SALESMAN: Yes. See.

MAN: Okay. You know what? I think I read this issue. Excellent issue. I couldn't put it down.

SALESMAN: Put it down, sir.

MAN: On the seat here. You want it?

SALESMAN: Yes.

MAN: Fine. If I hadn't read it, I'm sure this Fuchi Manuli would be sitting in my carport. Okay, I'll check you again when next week's *Time* magazine comes in.

SALESMAN: Or we'll call you.

MAN: Okay. Okay.

ANNCR: *Time.* The most colorful coverage of the week.

Time Magazine
"Train Station"
Used by permission of Dick Orkin and Bert Berdis

CONDUCTOR: [BG] All aboard!

VICTORIA: Darling, I can't let you go.

CHARLES: Victoria, it won't be forever.

VICTORIA: Oh, you'll write me every day, won't you?

CHARLES: Of course.

VICTORIA: Do you have the cookies I baked for you?

CHARLES: And the letter you wrote me to read on the train.

VICTORIA: Oh, Charles, one last embrace.

CHARLES: Victoria . . .

VICTORIA: Ohh . . . what's this in your coat?

CHARLES: Oh. It's *Time* magazine.

VICTORIA: Where did you get it?

CHARLES: Oh . . . I, heh heh . . . must have taken it from your apartment, silly.

VICTORIA: What?

CHARLES: I don't mean you, silly, I mean, silly I . . .

VICTORIA: Charles, that's *my Time* magazine.

CHARLES: I know, darling, but it's a long train ride and I wanted to read *Time*. It's so . . . me.

VICTORIA: Well, why didn't you buy your own *Time* magazine?

CHARLES: Darling, don't you want me to enjoy *Time*'s book reviews and theater section?

VICTORIA: But then I shan't be able to enjoy *Time*'s education section and [*English accent slips*] dance . . . [*accent again*] dance.

CONDUCTOR: All aboard!

SFX: [*Under*] [*Train steam hissing*]

CHARLES: Victoria, please, my train is about to leave.

VICTORIA: [*No accent*] Well, then, you better hurry and give me back my *Time*.

CHARLES: I can't believe this! You said your heart and soul belong to me.

VICTORIA: [*Tough-gal accent*] Well, my heart and soul are one thing, but I never threw in my *Time* magazine.

CHARLES: [*Receding into BG*] But I thought your *Time* was my *Time* . . .

VICTORIA: Oh, nice try, but no dice!

SFX: [*Locomotive engine starting to move*]

CHARLES: [*Frantic*] The train is leaving!

VICTORIA: Tough dogs!

CHARLES: Look, I'll pay you for the magazine. . . . It's not a big deal.

VICTORIA: No way José . . . you give me it back, you hear me!

ANNCR: *Time.* The most colorful coverage of the week.

Time Magazine
"Ripper"
Used by permission of Dick Orkin and Bert Berdis

BERT: Uh, pardon me, you almost finished with the *Time* magazine?

DICK: Uh, yeah.

BERT: It's the only one in the doctor's waiting room and I haven't read . . . so . . .

DICK: Well, as soon as I finish this *Time* article you can read it.

SFX: [*Rip*]

BERT: You're tearing the page there.

DICK: I just wanted this little science story here. See, it's very teeny.

BERT: Oh, okay . . .

DICK: . . . that I'm tearing out. That's all . . . then . . .

SFX: [*Long rip*]

BERT: Hey!

DICK: See, on the back of the *Time* science article is a
book review, but it's continued on this page. I'm
tearing this page out so as not to confuse you.

BERT: Don't . . . don't rip any more articles out of the
Time magazine, okay?

DICK: Okay.

SFX: [*Rip*]

DICK and BERT: Uh oh!

DICK: Darn, you know what I did?

BERT: You ripped another page.

DICK: I turned the page so quickly I tore out half this
really superb *Time* article on our economy.

BERT: That *Time,* you know, is for all sick people who
come in here, not just you.

DICK: Well, the page is hanging loose, so I better . . .

SFX: [*Rip*]

DICK: . . . before it hurts somebody.

BERT: All right, now that's it! You're being very selfish.

DICK: Oh, now, wait a minute. These aren't for me . . . these are for the, for my . . . uh . . .

BERT: Give me the magazine.

DICK: Okay . . .

BERT: I never miss the *Time* magazine movie review section. I want it.

DICK: Hey, if that's all you wanted, here . . .

SFX: [*Rip*]

BERT: I don't believe this.

DICK: What's a matter now? You want me to trim it for you? I can trim it. That's easy to do . . .

SFX: [*More ripping*]

BERT: That's not fair.

ANNCR: *Time* magazine. The most colorful coverage of the week.

⑦ Laughing Cow Cheese: Joy Golden Writes the Way People Really Talk

Client: Fromageries Bel/Laughing Cow Cheese
Agency: TBWA
Production Company: Joy Radio, Inc.
Date: 1984–1988

This is a story about three women, two men, and a cow.

From 1984 to 1988, radio listeners laughed at the continuing saga of a fast-talking Los Angeles Valley Girl and a nasal New York matron, the lead characters in a series of commercials for an imported French processed cheese brand called Laughing Cow.

The campaign was created for the TBWA agency in Manhattan by Joy Golden, a seasoned New York copywriter who was working part-time at the young up-and-coming agency. Led by President Richard Costello and Chairman Bill Tragos, the agency would later go on to be recognized for its legendary Absolut vodka print campaign. Golden had been brought in to work at TBWA by her friend, executive art director Carl Stewart, because of her strong background as a print writer. But that was soon to change.

Golden is the first of the characters in this story. Despite a long career that took her through many agencies in New York, Golden had never written any radio commercials. And as funny as Golden was, she had never used any comedy or humor in her ads. When she got the assignment, she thought, "a laughing cow in a red net bag, that's funny."

As with many advertising campaigns, serendipity, invention, and luck were behind the Laughing Cow commercials. The numerous awards given to the campaign are testimony to advertising that is genuinely human, written from real life, and deliciously relevant.

The Laughing Cow cheese brand, also known by its French name *La Vache Qui Rit,* was owned and marketed by the French company Fromageries Bel. The brand began in 1921 when Leon Bel registered the Laughing Cow icon. The cow with a "hilarious grin on its face" was based on a drawing done as an emblem for the "bus supplying fresh meat for the troops" during World War I, according to the company's web site. Over the years, the cow was used in various advertising and promotional campaigns for Fromageries Bel (FroBel) by both European and American advertising agencies.

Among its product lines of cheeses were Laughing Cow brand miniature processed snacking cheeses called Mini Babybel, Mini Bonbel, and Mini Gouda. They were packaged in yellow wax and sold in small red mesh bags. These little round cheeses hadn't been a heavily advertised product before 1983, when FroBel asked TBWA to come up with an advertising campaign to stimulate sales.

Costello recalled that the decision to use radio was a financial one. At $375,000—even in 1984 dollars—there weren't a lot of options for sustaining a presence in the media. In fact, the original plan was to advertise the French-branded processed cheese (which was actually made under license in the United States) in magazine ads because of the food's visual appeal. Though the agency hoped to show something more thrilling than a photo of cheese and crackers, they realized that the small budget wouldn't have much impact on their target demographic audience of women and single adults. To get the highest impact per dollar, the media director suggested radio. With limited product distribution, a local radio media buy in the New York metro area would not only help focus and optimize the budget, but would allow the Manhattan agency and New Jersey–based client to monitor the commercials' effectiveness in their own backyard.

Until that time, FroBel had not promoted the product much in the United States, partly because the FroBel U.S. advertising director at the time was poised for retirement and didn't want to rock the boat. When he left, FroBel replaced him with a new ad director from Europe: the younger, hipper Frank Schneiders. Recalling Schneiders, Costello said that the enthusiastic German loved American culture and humor and recognized that he would have to trust and depend on the agency to steer him in the right direction.

Because of her proven talent and status as a senior writer and creative director, Golden was given carte blanche on the assignment by Costello and Tragos. The agency account team showed Golden the product: three silver-dollar-size cheeses wrapped in yellow wax with a unique plastic zipper that split the wrapper in half. And, of course, the cheeses came packaged in the soon-to-be-famous red net bag. Originally branded simply as Babybel, Mini Bonbel, and Mini Gouda, Golden asked if she could call the product Laughing Cow cheese, translating from the French *La Vache Qui Rit*.

Enter the cow. Golden claimed she didn't know about the La Vache Qui Rit symbol or its history, so she didn't feel compelled to respect any sacred cows. Golden thought the idea of the mistaken wordplay about the cow was a great premise. For the demo spot, she wrote a commercial, which never ran, in which a woman in a supermarket asks the clerk to suggest a snack. "How about a Laughing Cow?" he says, and she replies, "It won't fit on a cracker," setting up the gag that would run throughout the 13-spot campaign Golden would eventually create.

In a 1989 interview in *Communications Arts* magazine, Golden said, "When I started doing these spots at TBWA, they just gave me the whole project. I went out and found the actors and the studio. I did the auditioning and the casting, from the creative concept out. I knew in my head what I was looking for, so I would be the only one who could know when I hit on it. I had the sense that in radio you really had to go for the voice, for the character. I knew—I guess instinctively—that the words were almost secondary to the performer."

In some ways, the radio media itself was in part responsible for creating the campaign. Golden's original thinking for the spots was to create a kind of "crazy New York lady" telling a rambling story about a cow and cheese. In her mind, she heard the nasal whine of Selma Diamond, a well-known comedienne who grew up in Brooklyn, where she took on the strong accent of a Jewish matron. Though she was a writer and an actress, Diamond later did stand-up comedy filled with sarcastic comments about the foibles of modern Manhattan *tsuris.* She was also well known for her late-in-life role on the television program, *Night Court.* Unfortunately, Diamond died of lung cancer in 1985, and Golden needed an actress who could capture her vocal sensibilities and rhythms.

In the casting studio, New York actress Lynn Lipton auditioned for one of the characters in the early spots. Golden remembers her as "very cute with sort of a Marilyn Monroe voice." Lipton asked if she could read for the character of Enid, the Jewish matron. "Should I do it ethnic?" Golden knew she didn't mean Canadian ethnic. "I thought," said Golden, "she means Jewish, and here I have a German client and a Greek agency president, but what the hell? When she did it, I knew I had a winner."

As a writer, Golden knew how the Enid character should talk, embodying women she had heard all her life as a New Yorker. Lynn Lipton, the actress who portrayed Enid, claimed she used her own mother as a referent when capturing the rhythms and timing of the character. Despite Golden's contention that Lipton's performance was the only element that brought the commercials to life, the writing is crisp, direct, and dazzlingly simple.

In the aptly named "Craving," the first of the Enid-character commercials, a woman recounts her husband's middle-of-the-night hunger for some cheese. "I'll go down to the all-night supermarket and get you a little round Laughing Cow in a red net bag," she tells him. And so begins the "Who's On First" Abbott-and-Costello-like wordplay that characterizes the entire campaign. The format allowed Golden to seamlessly slip the product names—Mini Babybel and Bonbel—into the character's idiosyncratic monologue, as well as copy points about the taste, location in the store, and packaging. In what would become the signature of the entire campaign, the spot ends with a zinger: Stuart tells Enid that the cheese was "the best treat he ever had in bed." She responds, "So I smacked him."

Golden was able to continue the story of Enid and her zany friends throughout the campaign by creating real-life food-oriented situations—parties, sweet-sixteen celebrations, brunches, or snack times. The device married creative entertainment and the necessary marketing sales pitch.

In another commercial, titled "Hot Tub Brunch," Enid is invited to "bring a little something" to her friend Bambi's hot tub party. In the pre-AIDS, swinging-singles era of the mid-1980s, a suburban hot tub party was considered the stuff of racy, elbow-nudging jokes. Telling Bambi that the cheese has an easy-open French zipper, the hot tub hostess replies, "Good, it's a kinky crowd anyway." Once again, Golden manages to work the copy points about the package into the context of the commercial, making it integral to the humor.

The spot ends with a line that captures Golden's sassy and sophisticated sense of humor: Bambi tells Enid that she has arranged for a live bull to be at the party as a date for the cow. "When I came out the cheese was gone. I said Bambi, I don't believe it, the bull ate the Laughing Cow. She said hurray for Hollywood."

The original $375,000 budget bought a 13-week test run consisting of 2,000 spots in the New York metro area. The commercials were an immediate success. Sales went up in New York about 62 percent, according to Costello. The disc jockeys started reporting that listeners were calling in to request the commercials, a phenomenon that has repeated itself time and again with popular commercials.

With the first year's creative and marketing success in 1984, FroBel's Schneiders was willing to virtually quadruple the budget to $1.3 million for 1985, rolling the campaign into other media markets where the product was distributed. Los Angeles was chosen next. But would the Jewish shtick that worked so well in New York play well in Los Angeles?

Golden thought so, considering the number of expatriate New Yorkers in California. But Costello wasn't so sure. He felt that campaign might need to be localized for the Los Angeles market, because its success in New York stemmed from the audience's recognition of the stereotype character of Enid. Golden admitted that beyond freeways, she didn't know much about Los Angeles. "For God's sake," Golden remembered Costello saying, "just don't do a Valley Girl character." What a great idea she thought. And thus Galaxy, the Valley Girl, was born.

The character of the Valley Girl had been popularized at the time by media mavens who noticed a type of slang "used by a narrow slice of the Los Angeles teen universe," according to Jason Salisbury, Internet writer reviewing the 1983 film *Valley Girl*. However, it was Moonunit Zappa, daughter of avant-garde rock composer/musician Frank Zappa, who released a novelty song in 1983 called "Valley Girl," in which she established the vocal caricature. Golden wanted to capture the same rhythm of a Valley Girl in her writing, so she listened to Zappa's record until she got a feel for the language.

True to her belief that the more human the character, the more the listener would identify with her, Golden imagined what would preoccupy the Valley Girl; Golden decided that a funny scenario would be to connect this 17-year-old boy-crazy girl with a California highway patrolman. Just as with Enid and her New Yorkisms, Galaxy the Valley Girl was all about cars, consumerism, California, and her "gorgoso" cop.

Golden was passionate about finding the rhythm of her character's speech patterns. Once she wrote the part, she knew that it would take the right actress to fully realize the character. "I had a feeling for the language," Golden said, "but the thing that's going to make this is . . . the right Valley Girl." Golden felt if she could find an actress who was young enough and hip enough she would bring some of her own rhythms and words to the reading. Just as she was lucky enough to find Lynn Lipton for the Enid character, Golden's unerring ear for casting the right talent found the perfect Los Angeles Valley Girl.

Over 125 actresses tried out for the part. One of them, according to Golden, was a "little chubby Jewish girl from Brooklyn, Julie Cohen." She nailed it in one take. Golden felt that Cohen's youth and familiarity with the character's quirks in men and shoes would bring Galaxy to life. Julie had the rhythms and the knowledge, even the ability to ad-lib the signature "okay" during the spots.

As with the Enid spots, Golden's ability to create a character that could communicate the product attributes and copy sales points makes the Valley Girl commercials a success. Galaxy's wall-to-wall words spin a spoofy tale of being stopped by a highway patrolman for speeding. Her excuse is that she is trying to get her Laughing Cow cheese, stored in the trunk, home quickly. And once again, the gag about cows, real and dairy, is off and running. In the following three commercials that featured Galaxy, she winds up dating the patrolman and eventually marrying him. Throughout all of them, Golden's knack for hearing her characters and capturing their quirkiness in her writing kept them funny, true, and credible.

As a radio writer, Golden put a lot of trust in her ears. She knew the kinds of voices she was looking for, heard them in her head, and then cast the actor who could bring the character to life. But creating great radio takes more than great writing. Fundamental to the radio copywriter's ability to write the script is the ability to cast and direct the actors. It's possible, according to Golden, to have really good copy ruined by a really bad actor. On the other hand, a good actor can save a mediocre commercial.

Despite Golden's initial lack of experience in writing funny radio commercials, her own exuberant character is the foundation of the Laughing Cow campaign. Even 15 years after the campaign ended, Golden's enthusiasm, spunkiness, and passion for her characters comes through.

As a supervisor and mentor to many younger writers throughout her career, Golden has much to offer. The lessons include the following:

1. Amuse yourself.

Golden had always wanted to write in the humorous vernacular that she would later capture so successfully that she was able to use it as a launching pad to a second career, setting up Joy Radio, an independent creative radio service that continues to this day. In advertising, writers are not often given the chance to do what they really want to do in service to the marketing strategy. By creating advertising that you would want to hear yourself and commercials that you would find funny, it's likely you'll try a bit harder. **Work that's done just to do the job won't have the same edge. Do what you want to do until it gets killed by somebody, says Golden, and it will really come out better.**

2. Be funny if you are.

Not everyone is born funny. Golden says, "If you're not funny, don't try to be funny." All comedy writers understand this maxim. All too often, a radio commercial will fall flat because the writer has tried to be funny when the subject or the copy doesn't warrant it or when the jokes are stale or trite. It's very difficult to learn to be funny; in fact, Golden believes that humor is instinctive. A sense of timing, of irony, of subversiveness—all are characteristics of a person who is funny.

Certainly, some techniques provoke humor better than others. For example, a surprise twist to produce an unexpected outcome can get a laugh. Golden uses this technique in the "Craving" commercial. Juxtaposition that contrasts the ridiculous with the serious works well in the "Hot Tub Brunch" spot. Exaggeration can make a point very silly, the way Galaxy's Valley Girl accent plays with language. But it takes practice to know how to employ these techniques. The surest way to find out if a spot is funny after you write it is to read it to someone you trust. "Not your mother," says Golden. Read it to other people and see if they laugh. If they do not, think about writing a serious spot. You can win awards that way, too.

3. Write the way people really talk.

It seems trite, but it really is a fact of life: All too often, radio copywriters are too busy putting "advertisingese" into the mouths of their characters. They stop being real people and become salespeople. It's very important to write the way people talk, says Golden, particularly on radio. People talk in dialogue that's very natural. They don't repeat each other's words just to emphasize the product name again and again. **Writing credible dialogue is an art. One effective technique is to eavesdrop on a conversation or record one that you're having, then play it back and transcribe the words just as you hear them. Realistic dialogue moves along with its own internal logic that grows out of the context of the conversation. People pause. They use fragments. They make assumptions that get them from one point to the next.**

4. Respect the talent.

Golden was able to get memorable performances from her actors in the Laughing Cow commercials because she was on the actor's side. She stresses the importance of not being adversarial when directing actors in a commercial. Coaxing a good reading means not dwelling on a bad reading.

"For example," Golden says, "you have to find how to encourage each actor, how to tease this one or kid that one" in order to improve his or her performance. "Without the actor," Golden continues, "you ain't got nothing!"

5. Be relevant.

The real secret to the success of the Laughing Cow commercials is their relevance. The copy points are so integrally woven into the jokes, stories, and gags that they become essential to the spot. Imagine the characters without their confusion about the cow. Observe how the product packaging is key to the progress of the story. **When creating a commercial, consider how the product will be used, who will use it, possible situations surrounding it, and just how far can you go with the idea. Golden connected the cheese with a variety of snacking situations that would allow her to make the jokes. The cardinal sin in radio copywriting is to disconnect the product as hero from the situation you create to amuse and entertain your listeners.**

Laughing Cow Cheese
"Valley Girl"
Used by permission of Joy Radio, Inc.

VALLEY GIRL #1: So like I was driving down the freeway, okay? And this totally gorgoso highway patrolman stops me. So I said like wow there's wheels on your motorcycle and wheels on my car. I mean that's like really kharmoso. He said you were speeding. I said I have to get my little round Laughing Cow in the red net bag into the fridge, okay? He said where's the cow? I said in the trunk, okay? He said you're not authorized to carry livestock. I said officer that is like really heavy.

The Laughing Cow isn't a real cow okay? It's cheese, okay? Mild Mini Bonbel. Nippy Mini Babybel. And new Mini Gouda. You know like really awesome and naturelle. Five round cheeses in little net bags. Each wrapped in wax with a cute little zip thing. He said open the trunk. I said okay. He said you need a key. I mean like this guy was like totally brilliant, okay? I said you want a little Laughing Cow? So he said okay. So I said okay. Okay. So we said okay. So then he asked me for my license. And I said when can I see you again? He was so totally freaked like he dropped the cheese and bit the ticket. So now it's like two weeks and like he never called.

Laughing Cow Cheese
"Craving"
Used by permission of Joy Radio, Inc.

ENID: Last night my husband woke me and said he had a little craving. I said I'll go down to the all-night supermarket and get you a little round Laughing Cow in a red net bag. He said I don't care if she's in lace with high heels, it isn't what I had in mind. I said what do you want, Stuart? He said something sort of soft and a little nippy. I said so you want Mini Babybel from the Laughing Cow? He said no. I said so you want Mini Bonbel? It's a little more mild. He said no. I said so what do you want, Stuart? He said cheese. I said what did you think I was talking about? So I went to the dairy case and I bought two red net bags with five minicheeses in each. Mini Bonbel and Mini Babybel. Delicious. Natural. Bite size. Then I went home and said look, Stuart, I brought you a little

Laughing Cow in a red net bag freshly wrapped in wax with an easy-open French zipper. He said, Enid, don't talk naughty to me. Then he ate all 10 minicheeses and said it was the best treat he ever had in bed. So I smacked him.

Laughing Cow Cheese
"Hot Tub Brunch"
Used by permission of Joy Radio, Inc.

ENID: Last Sunday my friend Bambi invited me to a hot tub brunch. I said good, I'll bring a little something. She said not Stuart. I said how about a little round Laughing Cow in a red net bag? She said forget it, I'm having 14, it won't fit in the tub. I said you don't put it in the tub. You put it on the table under the umbrella. She said if you're worried about sunburn, dump the red net bag and put the cow in a caftan. I said Bambi, your hot tub is running tepid. The Laughing Cow isn't a real cow, it's cheese. Mild Mini Bonbel. Nippy Mini Babybel. And new Mini Gouda. Five delicious natural bite-size cheeses in their own little net bags. Freshly wrapped in wax with an easy-open French zipper. She said good, it's a kinky crowd anyway. So I went to Bambi's brunch and what do I see? A big bull, complete with horns. She said it's for your laughing cow. This is a couple's party. So I put the minicheeses on the table and I went in the hot tub. When I came out the cheese was gone. I said, Bambi, I don't believe it, the bull ate the Laughing Cow. She said hurray for Hollywood.

Laughing Cow Cheese
"Valley Girl #3"
Used by permission of Joy Radio, Inc

VALLEY GIRL: Okay, so like I was sitting here eating a little round Laughing Cow in a red knit bag and counting how many pairs of shoes I owned when the telephone rang. I said like hello. And this deep voice said like hi. And then like I totally freaked. I said this isn't the highway patrolman? He said yes it is. I said no it isn't. He said yes it is. So I said really? Then he said like what're you doing? I said eating a little Laughing Cow and counting my shoes. He said got any extras? I said they're too small for you. He said that's okay, I eat 20 of them. I said even the suede ones? He said oh no. I said officer, why don't you come over and have the Laughing Cow instead? Mild Mini Bonbel. Nippy Mini Babybel. And smooth Mini Gouda. You know like really awesome and naturelle. Six delicious cheeses in little net bags. Each one wrapped in wax with a cute little zip thing. He said what's your address? I mean, talk about an inquisitive mind, right? I said you want crackers, too? He said okay. So I said okay. So okay, okay. So *then* I said what should we do after we eat the cheese? He said I'll watch you count your shoes. I mean like I've had heavy relationships before, but this is intense.

Laughing Cow Cheese
"Enid and Galaxy"
Used by permission of Joy Radio, Inc.

ENID: My daughter Tiffany invited to our home a girl named Galaxy who she met in Beverly Hills who wanted to see our eastern coast shopping malls. I said, hello Galaxy, she said . . .

GALAXY: Hi Tiffany's mother. I love your boots.

ENID: I said would you like something to eat or do you just shop? She said . . .

GALAXY: Oh no. I like love food, okay?

ENID: I said so how about a little round Laughing Cow in a red net bag? She said . . .

GALAXY: Oh . . . my . . . gosh! I can't believe foreigners eat Laughing Cow cheese like we do.

ENID: I said, Galaxy, I think there is a small cloud over your twinkling system. She said . . .

GALAXY: Tiffany's mother, that is like really poetry, okay?

ENID: I said, so would you like Mild Mini Bonbel, nippy Mini Babybel, Mini Gouda or what? She said . . .

GALAXY: Like, what's an "or what"?

ENID: I said, Galaxy, "or what" is a colloquism. She said . . .

GALAXY: Oh no, colloquisms give me boo-boos. I'll just have Mini Bonbel, okay. It's really awesome and naturelle.

ENID: I said, Galaxy, we pronounce it *natural*. Not *naturelle*. She said . . .

GALAXY: You are like so culturoso, really.

ENID: So we all had the Laughing Cow on crackers and Galaxy told me all about this highway patrolman she was in heavy lust with and after two hours of this I was like totally freaked okay.

⑧ Molson Beer: Anne Winn and Garrett Brown Understand Good Timing

Client: Molson/Martlett Importers
Agency: Rumrill-Hoyt/DFS/Lintas
Production Company: TwoVoices, Inc.
Date: 1981–1993

Radio is series of moments, a continuum of voices, music, and sounds connecting the seconds of a broadcast day. Radio advertising is sold in units of time; records designed for AM airplay were written to fit into a three-minute time slot; and even one of the most famous radio slogans of all time, created by Bob Klein of *Klein &* [*sic*] for Westinghouse's Group W's All News radio stations, promised to give listeners the world in 22 minutes. More so than newspapers, magazines, or possibly even television, radio has always been a medium of the moment, capturing news as it happens and responding to the events of the day. Radio advertising capitalizes on those moments to motivate listeners. Being timely, contemporary, and in touch with the moment helps radio advertisers sell.

Being in the moment in 1981 also helped Anne Winn and Garrett Brown sell a lot of Molson Golden beer and ale. Winn, a former copywriter, and Brown, an inventor and broadcast producer, created characters who sold the Canadian import by selling their own moments of witty banter and sexy repartee in a series of commercials they wrote and voiced for Molson. Though the campaign aired off and on during the next 12 years under the stewardship of three different advertising agencies, the incredible success of the Molson radio campaign can be attributed mostly to the verbal frisson between Winn's sophisticated, liberated woman and Brown's coolly hip man. Their conversations surrounding the beer captured a particular moment in contemporary social history when the two characters represented the qualities men wanted women to be and vice versa. It was a radio campaign that was truly right for the moment, and proof of that was that it didn't succeed until its time was right.

In the late 1960s, Winn and Brown were pursuing their careers at the Philadelphia advertising agency of Wermen & Schorr. Working as copywriters at nearby desks, the two were attracted to each other's wit and wordplay; according to Brown, Winn was the "funniest, most interesting talker" he'd ever met. As reported in an *Adweek* article in 1991, a colleague desperate for an idea in 1969 heard Winn and Brown trading wisecracks and convinced them to record a spot for a local clothing store. They then went on to record other commercials for various clients in the Philadelphia area, including Provident National Bank and a regional restaurant chain, the Brass Rail. In 1968, Wermen & Schorr was bought by the Rochester-based agency, Rumrill-Hoyt. Gene Novak, executive creative director and chairman of Rumrill-Hoyt, knew the spots Winn and Brown had done and asked them to do some demos for a couple of his clients, Michigan Bell and the Kodak radio network, in 1975. Novak liked the ad-libbed, improvisational quality of the Winn and Brown spots. At that time, Rumrill-Hoyt was the agency for the only U.S. distributor of Molson beer, located in Saratoga, New York. Even though the beer was widely popular in Canada, imported beers in the United States were just starting to catch on in the mid-1970s. Novak asked Winn and Brown to create a demo for his client, Martlett, the U.S. Molson distributor. As Winn recalled, "We ran down a half a dozen scenes after we started out with the basic scenario of a guy picking up a girl," adding that they wanted to do something believable and appealing, all surrounding beer.

The comparisons between the improvisational comedy of

Mike Nichols and Elaine May and Winn and Brown are hard to ignore. However, Nichols and May hadn't performed their skits at clubs or on record and television since quitting the scene in 1961. Their naturalistic moments of modern neuroses between men and women formed a legacy that Winn and Brown inherited.

Novak sensed the potential for the same kind of interplay between Winn and Brown. He liked the way the two created commercials that sounded like "overhearing a phone call . . . [the way] they step over each other's lines, they cough, stumble, and mispronounce, that's the intrigue." After several ad-libbed attempts, Winn and Brown recorded the first spot, called "Border Crossing," for Molson in 1975. It is literally an introduction of the Canadian beer to America, as Brown's Canadian beer truck driver attempts to cross the border into the United States and is stopped and questioned by Winn's zealous border guard on her first day on the job. Says Winn about the advertising strategic brief, "We took it quite literally, while not taking ourselves too seriously." Though the characters and interplay are a bit tentative and not fully realized in light of the other 35 spots they eventually recorded, the first commercial set the foundation for the future he-said/she-said format.

But that was in 1975, and the advertising executives of Molson felt that humor wouldn't sell beer. It was also the year Saigon fell to the Communists and the federal government had to bail out New York City; no one was laughing, and the world wasn't ready for funny, soft-selling beer advertising. So "Border Crossing," along with a couple of other spots that were recorded, were shelved.

Fast-forward five years. It's 1980 and times have changed. Reagan is in the White House. IBM launches the first PC. Princess Diana and Prince Charles are married. The economy is getting better. In the movies, a feisty, independent Margo Kidder as Lois Lane has encountered Christopher Reeve's sensitive Superman. Brooke Shields has offered a provocative glimpse of what comes between her and her Calvins. Men had evolved into sensitive New Age creatures, having had the macho beaten out of them by Vietnam. Alan Alda, symbol of the New Man and a dedicated feminist, had cochaired the Equal Rights Amendment Committee. By 1981, he was still caringly joking his way through *MASH*, the long-running hit television series. And on the show *Moonlighting,* which ran from 1985 to 1988, Cybil Shepard and Bruce Willis contemporized the same flirtatious banter that Winn and Brown were doing in their commercials for Molson and other products. With imported beers starting to catch on in the U.S. market, it was a particularly good moment to pitch to a new audience for beer—the women who made 30 percent of the beer purchases.

In 1981, Ray Shannon, vice president and brand director at Martlett Importers, Molson's U.S. distributor, had dusted off the "Border Crossing" spot and had Winn and Brown create about 10 others that were aired in limited markets working with Rumrill-Hoyt. The reaction was phenomenal. Disc jockeys talked up the commercials, and audiences responded by buying the beer.

But nothing can ruin success like success. With the growth of Molson in the United States, the distributor increased its advertising budgets with an eye to taking the campaign to a broader market through television. By 1984, Molson had changed its agency from Rumrill-Hoyt to Dancer Fitzgerald Sample, one of the world's largest agencies. Molson's "Border Crossing" spot was lost in the agency shuffle. Dancer naturally wanted to use its own creative executions; however, Shannon convinced the agency to play the Winn/Brown commercials in research focus groups to test against what was being proposed by the new ad agency. Winn remembers that the spots featuring the Molson Golden couple "blew everything else away." The "Border Crossing" spot received record scores with its portrayal of Winn's independent woman and Brown's cool dude. Terry Gallo, creative group head at Dancer, later commented that the

Molson campaign reflected "a new attitude in terms of the beer drinker. . . . People find this very appealing because they recognize themselves. . . ." Martlett wanted to revive the campaign, forcing the agency back into a strategy that would feature the radio commercials.

Continuing the campaign, however, meant convincing Winn and Brown to come back and create more commercials. By 1984, both of them had gotten out of advertising and were comfortably pursuing other careers. Brown had successfully developed the now famous and Oscar- and Emmy-winning STEADICAM®, and Winn was raising thoroughbred racehorses at her farm in Pennsylvania. At first, Brown tried sending the agency and Martlett to other radio production companies, such as Harley Flaum's Radio Band of America in Manhattan. But the more the Dancer agency played the "Border Crossing" spot in test groups, the more convinced the agency became that it wanted the pair to re-create their original magic. With Martlett geared up to spend $6 million on the campaign, the agency made Winn and Brown an offer they couldn't refuse: a huge creative fee plus triple the AFTRA union scale for their voice-over work and studio fees for a recording studio that Brown—with his engineering slant— hadn't even built yet!

The pair went on to create 15 commercials for Molson under Dancer's aegis. Ultimately, however, Dancer dropped the radio spots in favor of an ill-fated television campaign that tried to replicate the mystery and interchange of the characters. The concept included the gimmick of hiding the male and female character's faces but using Winn's and Brown's voices—it just didn't translate from radio to television. At the same time, Molson was also going through its own management shake-up, as it moved its corporate headquarters from North Hills, New York, to Reston, Virginia. By 1989, Winn remembers, Molson's importers had given their account to Lintas, a worldwide advertising agency, who also tried to push a television campaign. But Molson's new head of brand marketing, Peter Reaske, wanted to resurrect the radio campaign yet again. It was retested to convince Molson management—and the agency—that there was still fizz in the idea. In a case study written for Interep, the radio media sales company, Reaske said, "When consumers in focus groups were asked to recall beer ad campaigns, Molson is just as likely to appear in the top five as brands that spend millions on their advertising."

Molson began working directly with Winn and Brown, allowing Lintas only to choose media and provide marketing support, thus cutting the agency's creative fees. In an unusual move, the Molson contract with Winn and Brown included a sweetener that gave them a bonus for increases in cases of beer sold. However, by 1993, Winn recalled, with a new marketing VP on board at Molson, the account moved again, this time to Young & Rubicam, largely because Miller beer, a Y&R client, had picked up the now-lucrative U.S. license to distribute Molson. Winn and Brown were once again forced out, even though, nearly 12 years later, focus groups conducted by Y&R still registered the spots Winn and Brown had created.

The commercials for Molson that Winn and Brown created truly tapped into the zeitgeist of the 1980s. Winn was proud of her female character; as a copywriter, she was tired of seeing women in advertising portrayed as "a ditz or shrill." She finally had a chance to portray a real woman who was "reasonably intelligent." Winn's woman was more than equal to Brown's cool dude. "She didn't let me get away with anything. . . . I had to absolutely be at my best," he recalled. In an article in *Ads* magazine in June of 1985, writer Christina Kelly characterized the Molson spot as "a modern man and woman trading witticisms in contemporary settings . . . both . . . represented as fully developed, yet vulnerable human beings . . . in a campaign . . . that is revolutionary for a category whose typical backdrops run the gamut of traditional male activities."

Winn and Brown structured the process of writing, acting, and editing the spots to capture the precise moments of brilliance in their improvisational ad-libbing. According to Garrett, "What Anne and I managed to do was to find a way in the radio process that doesn't exist normally . . . to be ordinary in acting." By their own admission, the two weren't good enough actors to repeatedly pretend to respond to a joke in a convincing way. "But, by God," Brown said, "the first time she laughed at something I thought of, it's great."

The genesis of a Molson spot actually grew out of the informal guidelines of improvisational scene acting that Winn and Brown instinctively followed. Though Winn wasn't trained as an actress, she was a natural at the give-and-take exchanges— going with the flow of the interaction, listening and responding to the subtle changes in direction from the other—that are in fact the unwritten rules of improvisational theater. To start, Winn and Brown would devise a premise and a scene for each spot ahead of time, setting up different situations (a bar, a beach, a campground, a newly occupied apartment) that would inevitably lead to discussing beer. There were even some off-the-wall situations: two astronauts in a space capsule, two cops inventorying the loot from a heist, an outdoor rock concert, a guardian angel that leaves voice mail. Winn and Brown even did a spot called "Designated Driver" that promoted responsible drinking as well as pitching Molson beer. According to Brown, the "stuff that works the best . . . consists of the moment when the two participants meet. . . . neither know anything about the other and with anything possible . . . romance or marriage or life together." Quite simply, the two characters were always seduced by each other's wit and personality. Though Winn would sometimes come in "all steamed up" about a premise she had in her head, it often wouldn't play because she felt it was too "writerly" and lacked the apparent spontaneity of the other spots. "We'd have a lot of throw-outs," Winn recalled, "but the plots would cook over a week or so." Brown added that their challenge was always to plot a situation that would be about beer. True to good drama with some inherent conflict, the two would riff on a plot, verbally fencing back and forth until they had a perfect laugh, great repartee, and the right story.

That the commercials seemed like a spontaneous moment between the slyly flirtatious couple, was actually a testament to Brown's technical tour de force in editing. A gifted audio editor and engineer, Brown had designed the recording studio to allow him to capture the takes as they happened; there was no other engineer. Starting in the predigital days of sound recording, then later using the sound-editing software of Pro Tools, Brown would sometimes cut and paste as many as 60 electronic edits for a Molson spot. Says Brown, "We'd select these almost perfect moments, these encounters between two people."

Key to the spots is their sense of place. Whether it's in a crowded bar, at the U.S.-Canadian border, deep in the woods, or on a beach, listeners feel as though they are actually in the moment because of the highly complex mix of music and sound effects that Brown artfully created. "We would record in an absolutely acoustically dead room and I put back the acoustics for whatever the space was to be," he said. With sound effects and prerecorded music playing in their earphones, the process naturally forced Brown and Winn to speak louder or softer, faster or more languidly, depending on the commercial. The approach gave the commercials a sense of verisimilitude that brought realism to the moment. To listen to the commercials is to get a mental picture that makes Winn, Brown, and their environment all the more memorable.

"Border Crossing" set the tone for the rest of the campaign. In it, Winn's zealous U.S. Customs guard interrogates Brown's bewildered Molson beer truck driver. The listener can almost see her as she runs down the items on her clipboard, quizzing the driver about the contents of his Molson beer truck. "Any fruits or vegetables?" she asks officiously. "No," he stammers, "just Molson beer and ale." When she finds a six-pack of beer behind the driver's seat, she asks what it's for and he tells her it's a spare. The kicker comes when he confides that it is his first day on the job. "Mine, too!" she chimes back, and he offers her a beer, which she refuses, only to have him then try to give her an ale.

Though this first spot has many of the qualities that would later become signatures of the campaign—Winn's sexy, gentle laugh, Brown's bewildered yet singular focus on Molson beer, and a provocative premise designed to stimulate conversation specifically about the product—"Border Crossing" didn't yet have the sparkle of later spots such as "Designated Driver" and "Comedy Club."

"Designated Driver" is set, like many of the commercials, in a bar. We hear the ambience of the patrons as Winn's barmaid asks Brown's guy if he wants to order a drink. With the conversation-starting misunderstandings that are another hallmark of the spots, Brown says that he'd love a Molson, but he'd rather watch his friends drink them because he's the designated driver—a popular idea to prevent drunk driving, an issue that was gaining recognition in the national media through the efforts of the Harvard School of Public Health in 1988. Winn's character is drawn to this New Age man's admirable willingness to be the designated driver. He responds by asking her out. The spot has some of the best banter of the whole campaign, playing on the associations with the word *designated*. After he propositions her, Winn asks Brown if he's the "designated hitter." Saving the spot from becoming too treacly, she asks him at the end whether Brown's friends take turns driving so that he, too, can enjoy Molson, and he replies, "Sure, I'm a friend, not a saint." What also makes "Designated Driver" a standout among the spots is Brown's recording trick of mixing the bar sounds at just the right volume to have the listener imagine the character's voices are speaking a little too loud to be heard over the din.

Although many of the spots feature Brown as the instigator of the dramatic conflicts that propel the scenes, "Comedy Club" gives Winn a chance to be out in front. In the spot, she plays a female stand-up comic of the type who performed at the hundreds of comedy nightclubs that were springing up across the country. With comediennes such as Roseanne Barr, Brett Butler, Rita Rudner, and Ellen De Generes grabbing the spotlight in the mid-1980s, Winn and Brown capitalized on that moment to create the spot "Comedy Club." The commercial catches Winn's stand-up act in medias res as she bemoans the lack of marriageable men—a typical theme for many female comediennes. She singles out a guy in the audience, Brown, and puts him on the spot asking him to give his description of a perfect woman: "Tall, blonde, athletic, funny, warm, caring, giving, loving . . ." Of course, Winn's character doesn't miss a beat and says, "That's me!" She offers to buy him a beer for kidding him and, predictably, he's drinking a Molson. After a few lines about the beer, the spot ends with a bit of verbal play on Brown being more of an "imported" guy than a "domestic" guy. "The story of my life," Winn's comedienne concludes.

The success of the Molson campaign was so widespread that Brown and Winn were invited to teach radio and advertising professionals how to do funny commercials in far-flung locales like South Africa. Many of the lessons that they shared about writing for radio are applicable today. In fact, Brown's editing and technical lessons are particularly interesting to those creating radio commercials:

1. Sound different.

"You have to find a way to not sound like everything else that everyone is listening to," says Winn. The Molson spots were memorable because they didn't sound like the loud, cluttered commercials that were on the airways in the mid-1980s and early 1990s. The music was gentler, the dialogue more genuine. "Be real, be quieter than the level of the ambience . . . and give it some dead air—that really gets everybody's attention," Winn continues. **When creating a commercial, consider what else is out there competing with your message. A commercial**

that sounds like everything else will certainly be lost in the shuffle. Winn and Brown deliberately set out to create beer commercials that were 180 degrees different from other beer commercials—no macho guys, no homage to the purity of the water. It's important to sound different not only because your spots will be competing with other commercials, but also within the context of the programming environment. Will you be on a loud sports-talk radio show? Then speak softer. Does the media plan call for a smooth jazz format? Then go with the classics. "Give the spot some space to breathe," says Winn, and it will come to life.

2. Make the product the hero.
"If the product doesn't have some kind of reason to be involved in the commercial, you're in trouble," says Brown. **The sincerity and truthfulness of the Molson commercials comes through because each spot, regardless of where it is set, is about the beer that's being sold. The product is not incidental to the scene; it's about the beer, and everything else is just a vehicle to get to the pitch.** There must be a balance between the entertaining part of a spot—such as Winn and Brown's banter—and the information of the spot—the product pitch points. The Molson spots always cover the copy points of "fresh, clean taste." Everything else around them is there to make you believe those points. "Is the product in there because it has to be or because there is something interesting about it that you've found?" Brown questions. By making the product the hero around which all the action occurs, you'll have a more believable, enjoyable commercial.

3. Use the strength of radio—sound.
When creating a radio spot, remember that you are not writing a television commercial without pictures. Radio is a medium that is wholly dependent on the sounds you choose—the voices, the music, the special effects. As a sound engineer and broadcast producer, Brown worked very hard at making the spots

sound real. "I would record an ultrarealistic ambient sound . . . or buy it . . . and we would record to the actual music track or the ambient sound track and then mix it live." Many young copywriters aren't familiar with the capabilities of sound effects, having grown up in an era of television. **Find the best recording sound engineer you can and enlist his or her help in bringing your commercial to life with the best sound effects or music your budget can afford. Look for unusual sound effects that create images in your listeners' minds. Choose music that's different, unusual, or attention getting. You'll be strengthening your spots.**

Molson
"Border Crossing"
Used by permission of TwoVoices, Inc.

MUSIC: [*Under*]

SFX: [*Outdoors*]

SFX: [*Truck comes to a stop*]

BORDER GUARD: Citizen of . . . ?

MOLSON DRIVER: Ah . . . Canada.

BORDER GUARD: Contents of the truck?

MOLSON DRIVER: Yes!

BORDER GUARD: What do you mean, yes?

MOLSON DRIVER: It's ah . . . *Yes.* . . . It's full of Molson beer and ale, like it says on the side. . . . My truck's full of Molson beer and ale!

BORDER GUARD: Destination?

MOLSON DRIVER: Uh, United States. We bring Molson beer and ale into the United States every day . . . fresh, clean taste of . . . Molson's, with a taste as big as Canada . . . you've heard of Molson. . . .

BORDER GUARD: All right. Out of the truck!

MOLSON DRIVER: Out of the truck?

BORDER GUARD: Any fruits or vegetables?

MOLSON DRIVER: No . . . just beer and ale, like it says on the side.

BORDER GUARD: Is this for your personal consumption?

MOLSON DRIVER: Yes . . . *no.* It's for your, all your personal consumption down in the United States.

BORDER GUARD: All right, what's behind the seat?

MOLSON DRIVER: Behind the seat . . . ah, just the whole rest of the truck.

BORDER GUARD: No, No, behind the seat!

MOLSON DRIVER: Oh, it's just a spare . . . six-pack . . . for later.

BORDER GUARD: Aha!

MOLSON DRIVER: Aha?

[*Laughs*]

ANNCR: Molson Golden and Molson Light. Since 1786, pure and simple. Molson is Canadian beer. Imported by Martlettt—Reston, Virginia.

MOLSON DRIVER: Look it's just my first day . . . I don't know what's happening . . .

BORDER GUARD: Mine, too.

MOLSON DRIVER: Yours? You want a beer?

BORDER GUARD: I don't think I can accept one.

MOLSON DRIVER: How about an ale?

[*Laughs*]

Molson
"Designated Driver"
Used by permission of TwoVoices, Inc.

SFX: [BG] [*Bar sounds/laughter/talking/music*]

BARMAID: Hi, can I get you something?

DESIGNATED DRIVER: Oh, ah . . . no, not really.

BARMAID: You're not drinking?

DESIGNATED DRIVER: I'd love a Molson.

BARMAID: That's easy enough, I'll just go and . . .

DESIGNATED DRIVER: No, no, I just want to love it, I don't want to have one, you know what I mean . . .

BARMAID: Really, Why?

DESIGNATED DRIVER: I just like talking about it . . . cool, clear, imported from Canada. . . . I'm watching a few of them over there. . . . Molson Golden . . .

BARMAID: Uh, yeah, I know . . . those are all your buddies, right? How come, uh . . .

DESIGNATED DRIVER: Oh yeah, I'm watching them, too . . . yeah, no, I'm the . . . uh . . . driver . . . I'm the . . . I'm the . . .

BARMAID: . . . the designated driver?

DESIGNATED DRIVER: I am . . . very designated . . . that's right . . . uh . . .

BARMAID: Oh yeah . . . and . . . and what are they, the designated drinkers? [*Laughs*]

DESIGNATED DRIVER: That's right . . . I [*unctuously*] . . . I'm driving them home . . . [*interspersed*] . . . I'm being very good . . .

BARMAID: Ahhh . . . that's real . . . you're a . . . you're a good friend . . .

DESIGNATED DRIVER: Do you admire me very much?

BARMAID: Yes, definitely. I think that's very admirable . . .

DESIGNATED DRIVER [*With mock humility*]: Can I take you for a ride? Designate me! Quick!

BARMAID: [*Laughs*] . . . I see you're the designated hitter, too!

DESIGNATED DRIVER: Oh yeah! . . . [*laughs*]

ANNCR: Molson Golden and Molson Light. Since 1786, pure and simple. Molson is Canadian beer. Imported by Martlettt, Reston, Virginia.

BARMAID: So do you guys take turns?

DESIGNATED DRIVER: Uh, hitting?

BARMAID: No! *Driving.*

DESIGNATED DRIVER: Yeah, sure, I'm a friend, I'm not a saint . . . you know.

    (*Laughs . . . fades out*)

Molson Golden
"Comedy Club"
Used by permission of TwoVoices, Inc.

SFX: [*Laughter/intimate Comedy Club ambience*]

STAND-UP: This is what I believe . . .

[*laughs as appropriate, including from "the audience guy"*]

STAND-UP: . . . the year I was born, Martian women came and stole all the male babies . . . really . . . except for one . . . and he happens to be here tonight . . . put the spotlight on this guy . . .

AUDIENCE GUY: Uh-oh . . . oh no . . . ah . . . don't do this . . .

STAND-UP: . . . the last available man on earth . . . nice looking . . . what's the matter? No date tonight?

AUDIENCE GUY: Well . . .

STAND-UP: What *are* you looking for in a woman anyway? . . . we want to know . . . yeah . . .

AUDIENCE GUY: Really? Uh, tall, blonde, athletic..

STAND-UP: Ah, like me! . . . me!

AUDIENCE GUY: Yeah, beautiful, brilliant, you know, the usual . . . funny, warm, caring, giving, loving . . .

STAND-UP: [*interspersed*] . . . this is amazing . . .

AUDIENCE GUY: . . . rich!

STAND-UP: . . . he wants me! Let me buy you a beer. What are you drinking?

[*unison*] Molson Golden!

AUDIENCE GUY: Yeah, sure!

[*unison*] Molson Golden!

STAND-UP: Oh, great beer . . . he's smooth, he's cool . . . You're the imported type?

AUDIENCE GUY: What?

STAND-UP: You're the imported type?

AUDIENCE GUY: Ah . . . I'm not the domestic type.

STAND-UP: Oh no . . . you see . . . [*laughter*]

ANNCR: Molson Golden and Molson Light. . . .

STAND-UP: . . . it's always something.

ANNCR: Since 1786, pure and simple. Molson is Canadian Beer. Imported by Marltett Reston, Virginia.

STAND-UP: . . . story of my life.

AUDIENCE GUY: I am housebroken! [*takes her by surprise, big laughs, fx fades*]

⑨ Motel 6: The Richards Group Leaves a Light On for the Brand

Client: Motel 6, Accor Economy Lodging
Agency: The Richards Group
Production Company: The Richards Group/In-house
Date: 1986–present

With the first few notes of a slightly out-of-tune fiddle, the plunking traveling music of a guitar, and the folksy greeting of Tom Bodett, listeners instantly recognize the radio campaign for Motel 6 that has been running for the past 15 years. Named by *Advertising Age* magazine as one of the top 100 ad campaigns in history, the Motel 6 radio commercials—over 1,000 produced to date—are an advertising anomaly because of their remarkable longevity and consistency. Far from the jokes or belly laughs of other humorous radio campaigns, the Motel 6 commercials offer winsome wit and a gentle smile.

Launched in 1986, the Motel 6 radio campaign was created by The Richards Group advertising agency, headquartered in Dallas, Texas. Despite changes in personnel at both client and agency over the years, the radio campaign is a study in classic branding and smart marketing that has helped maintain the style, messages, and distinctiveness of the commercials for nearly two decades. No one connected with the creative product at the start suspected that the commercials would be the long-running success they have become—in terms of both their numerous advertising awards and the increased business for Motel 6. However, the individual decisions, from branding strategies to musical styles, have kept the Motel 6 radio commercials fresh, compelling, and one of the most memorable campaigns in advertising history.

In 1986, the Motel 6 chain, which offered $6 per night economy lodgings, was owned by KKR, the financial investment group whose corporate acquisitions in the mid-1980s characterized the tenor of the go-go years of Reaganomics. However, despite its investment in the chain, occupancy rates for the 200 Motel 6 locations scattered around the country were in a downtrend, dropping 2 percent per year. In March of 1986, the CEO of Motel 6, Joe McCarthy, turned for help to Stan Richards, principal of The Richards Group, which had been the agency for Lincoln Properties, McCarthy's previous company.

Stan Richards founded The Richards Group in 1975, transforming a "minuscule creative boutique into a national-scale branding agency with a staff of over 500 and billings over $600 million today," according to the agency's corporate history. One of the most recognized and honored advertising professionals in the Southwest, Richards eventually enlisted Rod Underhill, brand group head, to work with Hugh Thrasher, Motel 6's executive vice president of marketing and development.

At that time, the Motel 6 properties were scattered across the country, with a heavier concentration in California and Texas, and they represented a mixed bag of economy lodgings, lacking telephones in the rooms and requiring payment to unlock television controls. Although Motel 6 could boast of having the lowest price of any national chain, The Richards Group recognized that the brand's point of difference—frugality—was a tough sell in an era when conspicuous spending from the 1980s Wall Street boom was still the norm . . . that is, until the economic bubble burst in October of 1987 and the fat Mont Blanc Meisterstück fountain pens used to sign merger and acquisition deals were now signing unemployment checks. But the typical Motel 6 customers—traveling salespeople, families on budgets, retired adults—didn't want to seem cheap when choosing economy lodging. Wisely, The Richards Group, known for its expertise in strategic branding, determined after extensive research that the best positioning for Motel 6 was to cast the chain as one that "provides frugal people with a comfortable place to stay at the lowest price of any national chain." Instead of being cheap, lodgers at Motel 6 were dubbed "smart." After all, who needed fancy amenities when you were just looking for a clean, comfortable place to sleep for one night. The brand's personality was described by The Richards Group as "honest, simple, friendly and fun. Humble and unpretentious. Good-humored and common-sensical."

Research also revealed that these targeted frugal people "made the decision to stay through the windshield of their cars," according to Underhill; most travelers arrived without a reservation. Additionally, Underhill added, the typical advertising for the lodging industry was to show the room in television commercials, which was a decided disadvantage for Motel 6's spartan accommodations. Those two facts, along with a limited $1 million budget for the first year, drove the advertising agency's decision to recommend a blitz of concentrated radio commercials in 1986.

The task of creative development fell to David Fowler, a creative group head and senior writer at The Richards Group. Fowler understood from the strategic brief and the meeting with the client that the commercials needed to reflect the brand personality by being as simple, straightforward, and plainly honest as a room in a Motel 6. "I realized that I had to tell the truth about the motel chain. Telling people that we just installed phones and free TV in our motel rooms . . . either the audience was going to laugh at us or with us. We thought it was best to laugh with us," recalled Fowler. In 1991, Motel 6 was acquired by French-owned Accor, the world's largest accommodations company. Accor's infusion of over $600 million into property renovations and improvements—including telephones in every room—not only revived the properties themselves, but also provided fodder for new commercials.

Like most agencies, The Richards Group wanted to do focused research group tests as a guide in choosing the best creative approach. Fowler suggested three possible spokespeople for the campaign. First was the Smothers Brothers comedy duo, whose gentle humor and down-home appeal made them highly popular recording artists, performers, and satirical TV hosts in the 1960s. The second alternative spokesperson for whom Fowler wrote a sample script was Mal Sharpe, the well-known man-on-the-street reporter whose simple but zany style of greeting traveling strangers also fit the fun personality of the Motel 6 brand. Last, Fowler was interested in the possibility of using Tom Bodett, a little-known radio commentator, humorist, and writer whose singsong vocal cadence and homespun humility on National Public Radio's *All Things Considered* program had captured Fowler's attention a year earlier (when NPR was the only station Fowler could get on the broken tuner in his old pickup truck). Impressed, Fowler called Bodett at his home in Alaska one day in 1985 and asked for a sample tape of NPR broadcasts to keep in his files.

Fowler wrote several scripts and descriptions of each of the possible spokespeople for qualitative focus groups. The results of the focus research, Underhill recalled, startled the agency. "It was a good lesson in the principle that a spokesperson should reflect an entity that your prospects and customers really believe use the product." No one in the focus groups believed for a minute that Dick and Tommy Smothers would stay in a Motel 6. Few warmed to Mal Sharpe's script. However, about half the people who heard the demo spots liked what Thomas Hripko, the second Richards Group writer/producer/director of the Motel 6 campaign, called Bodett's "guy-next-door believability." The other half of the people, Underhill remembered, thought Bodett was "stupid, folksy, and corny." Thankfully, Motel 6's marketing director Hugh Thrasher had the guts to go forward with the campaign using Bodett.

Fowler approached Bodett about being the spokesperson for the motel chain. Remarkably, for a voice and name that has become synonymous with a famous advertising campaign, Bodett was hesitant to do the commercials; as a published author and NPR contributor, Bodett was worried about potential conflicts of interest that might taint his career. He asked a colleague at National Public Radio if he should accept the offer. The colleague answered, "How much are they going to pay you?"

With Bodett's voice clearly in mind, Fowler realized the importance of background music to the announcer's folksy delivery. Taking the audiotape that Bodett had sent him of his NPR piece on the disappearance of socks from clothes dryers, Fowler went to Dallas composer and musician Tom Faulkner. "Originally," Faulkner remembered, "Dave knew he wanted traveling music, but he wanted something like a symphony." Fortunately for Motel 6, rather than using musical juxtaposition, Faulkner suggested framing Bodett's voice with music that would reinforce it—something simple, like acoustic traveling music. Besides, on a tight budget, a full symphony would be out of the question.

True to the Motel 6 brand personality, Faulkner called on his own experiences of staying in Motel 6 rooms and his intuitive understanding of the brand's personality. He told Fowler that he thought the music should be plain and simple, just like the lodging. Fowler gave Faulkner the freedom to pursue what he heard in his head—a 60-second sound track to a travelogue, something like a little car "putt-putting down the highway on its way to Motel 6." That gave Faulkner the 4/4 rhythm that he put into the guitar part. The melody, according to Faulkner, was composed in just one hour instead of his usual two to seven days. Faulkner called in longtime friend and musician Milo Deering to do the fiddle part, "slightly out of tune in the key of A." Over the years, there have been attempts to freshen up the music—including one using a version of an oompah band—

but wisely, Motel 6 marketing executives have decided to stick with the original folksy melody as part of the audio brand strategy.

Of the more than 1,000 Motel 6 commercials produced to date, all follow the same format created by Fowler in 1986 with the first commercial, "Comparison #2," a wry point-by-point comparison between Motel 6 and "fancy hotels." As the spot says, "They have beds, we have beds." What Motel 6 didn't offer was "avocado body balm," an amenity Fowler thought sounded funny enough to include in the copy. Fowler worked on the campaign long enough to create the first 19 commercials (1986 through 1987) before leaving The Richards Group. He handed over the reins to Thomas Hripko, who continued the format, creating another 300 spots over six years by drawing on his own small-town Texas experiences (until his own departure from The Richards Group in 1992).

Fowler knew the spots would continue to roll out, so he created a simple template that contained most of the basic copy points of the marketing strategy. After some tweaking, the line became: "We're the lowest priced of any national chain, around 20 bucks in most places, a little less in some, a little more in others, but always a heck of a deal for a clean, comfortable room." Beyond that, the writers who followed Fowler—from Hripko to Mike Renfro, Mike Bales to David Longfield, and dozens of others whose ideas were turned into commercials over 15 years—dressed the copy messages in their own ideas. Even though Stan Richards has handpicked the dynasty of talented writers most appropriate for the Motel 6 client, the hundreds and hundreds of spots have remained remarkably similar.

Certainly, Bodett's reading has a lot to do with the continuity. But as Fowler and Hripko put it, the best spots over the years have been written to accentuate the natural rhythm of Bodett's pacing, cadence, and breath in the service of telling the story. Even from the start, Fowler recognized that the scripts had to be perfectly written for Bodett to read, because there would be no editing out the unwanted recorded breaths, a practice common in most announcer-read commercials.

According to Fowler and Hripko, the recording sessions weren't really like work, "more like a bunch of friends hanging out together and recording this stuff." Structured to accommodate Bodett's peripatetic lifestyle and residence in Homer, Alaska, a batch of 10 to 12 commercials was recorded every quarter during the year in studios in San Francisco, Seattle, and eventually Alaska, where Bodett later built his own recording studio in his home. All the spots were engineered by Bob Lindner, the original sound engineer from San Francisco's Coast Recording. The laid-back feeling captured in the spots was a product of Bodett's typical routine: becoming familiar with each new set of scripts on the day of a recording session, breaking for a bit of lunch, and recording the final take in an afternoon session. Bodett would read along to the now-famous music to help him with his pacing, as do many voice-over announcers. His guy-next-door believability and earnest, friendly frugality come through in every spot. In fact, according to Eric Studer, senior vice president of marketing for Accor Lodging North America, research has shown that people identify Bodett with their own frugal personae, whether they are young or old, black or white. (Even a New York cabbie saw Bodett as "my man, Tom.")

The charm of the commercials grows directly out of their honesty and simplicity. Even the famous tag line—"We'll leave a light on for you"—was the result of the brand attributes. The first few commercials carried no tag line. Then, during one session, the team had finished recording a spot Fowler had underwritten: It was only 56 seconds long, not the 60 seconds required for radio station airplay. A little recording booth discussion ensued and various ideas were suggested. Among them, Bodett suggested a phrase his mother used to say to him when she was worried about his coming home late. "I'll leave the light on for you," was what she said, and Bodett offered it, among other solutions, as a four-second tag line. Not only did it reflect the vacancy light of the motels, but it also captured the feeling of a friendly welcome. When Fowler returned to play the tapes for his boss's approval, Richards wisely selected "leaving the light on" in every spot. It became a signature line for the entire 1,000-plus commercials in the campaign.

Keeping the campaign fresh has been a challenge met by every writer in The Richards Group. Many spots have been needed because of the heavy media schedule; Richards, concerned that with intense airplay the spots would get tired, made sure they were rotated often, which necessitated a constant bank of new commercials.

The types of commercials seem to fall into three categories that reflect the evolution of the marketing strategy. Basic spots reinforce the Motel 6 brand features of lower price and clean rooms, differentiating the chain from its competition with humorous comparisons. "Comparison #2," the first commercial written for the campaign and recorded on August 4, 1986, exemplifies this type of spot: In the commercial, Bodett compares Motel 6 to fancy hotels with higher prices. "They've got sinks and showers; by golly, we've got 'em, too," Bodett states. He continues the comparison by saying what Motel 6 *doesn't* have: French-milled soap or avocado body balm. In fact, it is Bodett's reading that carries the commonsensical positioning of the brand; who can argue with a man who sounds so earnest and plainspoken?

The second type of commercial plays around with topicality. It's an easy way to keep the commercials fresh, drawing on news of the day (presidential elections, local market events, the 1995 major league baseball strike). In "Deficit Reduction," Bodett offers his "open letter to the president" (at that time Bill Clinton). In the spot, written by Hripko, Bodett suggests that staying at Motel 6 can be a way for the president and "those guys in the suits and dark glasses that follow you" to help shrink the deficit. Again, the comparisons are made with the "big fancy places" and their "guava-gel conditioning shampoo." The kicker at the end of the spot chides President Clinton for the infamous $150 dollar haircut he received while visiting Los Angeles. "I'd say you probably spent enough money on your hair, anyway." And in a tiny tweak to the tag line in deference to the commander in chief, Bodett finishes, "We'll leave the light on for you, *sir.*"

Finally, there are the spots that stand out for their unique and gentle silliness. Making balloon animals on the radio in the shape of the St. Louis skyline, for instance, was done to help pitch business locally in Missouri. Another spot, which won the $100,000 grand prize at the Radio-Mercury Awards for Hripko in 1992, was titled "Singing Phone Number." Motel 6 marketing director Thrasher had come to Motel 6 from the Hyatt chain, where he had once overseen a big Busby Berkeley–type commercial that featured a marching band spelling out the 800 reservation number for Hyatt. To celebrate Motel 6 finally getting its own 800 number, Thrasher wanted The Richards Group to do its own "big production" spot, but in the down-to-earth Motel 6 style.

Hripko created a jokey concept that had Bodett singing the phone number, an idea that embarrassed the shy announcer. Persuading him to do it as a gag for Thrasher and as a gift to Hripko on his birthday, Bodett finally relented and used his embarrassment as an endearing quality. In fact, in the copy, he says, "I told them I didn't want to do this, but they insisted, so here goes." In fact, the ending of the spot was changed from "We'll leave the light on for you," to "I'm Tom Bodett, and, boy, am I embarrassed." Thrasher was overwhelmed with laughter and insisted that the spot run. And it walked away with the Radio-Mercury Award.

Advertising judges have lauded the campaign for years— virtually every Radio-Mercury Awards competition has had a Motel 6 commercial in the finalist category. The ads have also won Effies, Clios, ADDYs, One Show awards, and many other local and national accolades (among which was a Clio for its public service announcement on drunk driving). The public has also appreciated the campaign, sending in a constant stream of fan letters to Bodett, Motel 6, and The Richards Group.

The campaign has also worked. Occupancy in Motel 6 properties went up 7 percent in the first year, the highest gain ever recorded in the industry. Even with an advertising budget that to date has never exceeded one-tenth of what Holiday Inn spends per year, Motel 6 advertising continues to score an increasingly huge lead in unaided recall over other economy lodging chains.

That success offers valuable lessons for copywriters, agency account people, and client advertising managers:

1. Know your brand's personality.

The original strategic brief created by The Richards Group aptly characterized the attributes of the Motel 6 brand personality. That simple, down-to-earth unpretentiousness became the guiding foundation for everything from the copy to the music to Bodett's voice. "Once I knew who the character was, it was some of the simplest writing ever," said Fowler. And Thrasher's acknowledgment of Motel 6's spartan proposition allowed the agency and the audience to laugh with it. Even Faulkner's musical signature captures the experience of the road-weary budget traveler "putt-putting" down the road through the guitar rhythm and the longing of the fiddle's melody. **Be honest about your brand's personality. Accept its unique character and quirks, and portray them truthfully through all the elements of the radio production.**

2. Talk *to* your audience, not at them.

By labeling Motel 6's customers "smart and frugal" instead of cheap, The Richards Group spoke to the audience's

innermost insecurities. "The magic in creating a contagious campaign is understanding how to be really relevant to the people you're trying to influence," says Underhill. Talking plainly to their need for a clean, comfortable, inexpensive room and recognizing the simple needs of legions of traveling salespeople, retirees, and budget travelers is one of the keys to the success of these commercials. The single, earnest voice of Bodett literally speaks directly to the audience, as research and time have shown. Blasting listeners with only client-directed copy points ignores their ability to simply change the station. If you want someone to listen to you, talk *to* them, not at them.

3. Do your own research.

Although focus groups and artificial consumer research have killed more than one good campaign, both The Richards Group executives and Motel 6 management were smart enough to trust their instincts and take a minimal risk when the initial feedback on Bodett was less than 100 percent acceptance. But that wasn't the only kind of research that contributed to the success of the campaign. At one time or another, composer Faulkner and writers Fowler and Hripko had stayed at Motel 6 as paying patrons. Their own experiences of staying at Motel 6 properties, whether talking to people at the ice machine or by the pool or visiting with their kids and in-laws, found their way into the actual commercials. Their personal research brought reality and truth, not to mention a few smiles, to the scripts. **Find out about your clients. Use their products. Visit their stores and offices. Talk to real people about how they use the products. Gather your own body of knowledge to balance what you hear in focus groups—and you just might have the same kind of success that keeps the light on at Motel 6.**

Motel 6
"Comparison #2"
Used by permission of Accor Lodging North America

TOM: Hi. Tom Bodett for Motel 6 with a comparison.
You know, in some ways, a Motel 6 reminds me of
those big fancy hotels. They've got beds; we've got
beds. They've got sinks and showers; by golly, we've
got 'em, too. There are differences, though. You can't
get a hot facial mudpack at Motel 6 like at those fancy
joints. And you won't find French-milled soap or
avocado body balm. You will, however, get a clean,
comfortable room for the lowest prices of any national
chain. Motel 6 has over 750 locations from coast to
coast, and they're always a heck of a deal. Oh sure, it'll
be rough to survive one night without avocado body
balm or French-milled soap, but maybe the money you
save'll help get you over it. It always works for me.
Well, call 1-800-4-MOTEL-6 for reservations. I'm
Tom Bodett for Motel 6, and we'll leave the light on
for you.

Motel 6
"Deficit Reduction"
Used by permission of Accor Lodging North America

TOM: Hi. Tom Bodett for Motel 6 with an open letter to
the president. Well sir, you asked us all to contribute to
help shrinking the deficit. And since what's good for
the goose is good for the gander, I've got a painless
way for you to contribute along with the rest of us—
Motel 6. Instead of staying at those big fancy places

when you go out on business, you could stay at the Six. You'd get a clean, comfortable room for the lowest prices of any national chain and a good night's sleep to go along with it. Those guys in the suits and dark glasses that follow you around could stay in the room with you for just a few extra dollars. Heck, maybe you could all watch a free in-room movie or make a few free local phone calls or something. It'd be a blast. Oh sure, you'd have to do without a shower cap and that fancy guava-gel conditioning shampoo, but all in all, Mr. President, I'd say you've probably spent enough money on your hair, anyway. I'm Tom Bodett for Motel 6, and we'll leave the light on for you, sir.

Motel 6
"Strike 3"
Used by permission of Accor Lodging North America

TOM: Hi. Tom Bodett for Motel 6 with some thoughts about the big baseball strike. You know, a lot of the players are probably using this time off to take a rare summer getaway. And with those million-dollar salaries on hold, it only makes sense that they stay at Motel 6. Of course, they wouldn't get the pampering they're used to at those big fancy hotels, but they would get a clean, comfortable room for the lowest prices of any national chain. And since the owners aren't exactly making money hand over fist right now, they could stay at Motel 6 on their vacations, too. Well, just picture it—they run into the players down at the ice machine and hang out together watching free in-room movies, like that heartwarming one where that guy builds a ballpark in his cornfield. Everybody gets all misty-eyed and they sit down and settle their differences right then and there. Could happen. I'm Tom Bodett, part-time mediator, for Motel 6, and we'll leave the light on for you.

Motel 6
"Aunt Josephine"
Used by permission of Accor Lodging North America

TOM: Hi. Tom Bodett for Motel 6 with good news for the traveler. Well, it's time for the biannual trip to see Aunt Josephine. She's a wonderful lady, but the only problem is her cats. It never fails, the moment you step in the door, the big black one, Muffie, starts that curling thing around your leg, and for the rest of your stay you're doomed to be the object of Muffie's desire. Well, it makes it hard to concentrate on Aunt Josephine's story about Mildred's cousin's husband's neighbor, who just had her goiter treated. But maybe I got a way to get you off the hook with Muffie. Motel 6. We'll give you a clean, comfortable room for the lowest prides of any national chain. Plus you get free local phone calls and there is no motel service charge on long-distance ones. And, at Motel 6, you'll never wake up to find Muffie flipping her tail in your face. Personally, that's worth the price of the room right there. I'm Tom Bodett for Motel 6, and we'll leave the light on for you.

> ## Motel 6
> ## "Financial Guru"
> ### Used by permission of Accor Lodging North America

TOM: How to make a million dollars with no money down? Sort of. Tom Bodett here for Motel 6. Well, those get-rich-quick guys are everywhere, so I thought I'd get into the act, too. I've got my aloha shirt on and a foolproof one-step program that'll put money straight into your pocket. You won't believe how easy it is. Instead of dropping a bundle at one of those fancy joints, come stay at Motel 6 and pocket the difference. You get a clean, comfortable room for the lowest prices of any national chain. In the morning, you won't have a million dollars, but you will have a nice chunk of change left over. And to think, you got all this great advice without even having to attend my seminar. Well, call 1-800-4-MOTEL 6 for reservations. And remember, think positive, control your destiny, and buy my video. I'm Tom Bodett, financial guru for Motel 6. We'll leave the light on for you.

⑩ Ortho Antstop Fire Ant Killer: Radio Savant Goes Straight for the Announcer

Client: Ortho Antstop Orthene Fire Ant Killer
Agency: BBDO West
Production Company: Radio Savant
Date: 1996–1997

I t is almost impossible not to laugh at the radio commercials for Antstop Orthene Fire Ant Killer from Ortho. The campaign for this powerful specialized insecticide was created in 1996 and 1997 by Radio Savant, a Los Angeles creative production company run by the husband-and-wife team of April Winchell and Mick Kuisel. Listeners laughed so hard they wanted to hear more of the macabre humor. The Ortho clients laughed as the commercials racked up record sales. Even the judges at the Radio Advertising Bureau's Radio-Mercury Awards laughed, handing Radio Savant $100,000 in prize money. About the only people who didn't laugh were representatives of People for Ethical Treatment of Animals (PETA). But then, PETA members probably were never bitten by fire ants.

It was an unusually wet and warm spring in Texas in 1996, perfect conditions for fire ants to build their mounds and bite any living creature that got too close. And although local residents of the South and Southwest have all kinds of home remedies for getting rid of the pestilent fire ants, from drowning them in a mix of grits and water to setting their mounds ablaze with gasoline, Antstop Orthene® Fire Ant Killer from Ortho offers a far easier and more effective solution.

Ortho's advertising agency, BBDO West, had handled the company's broad line of lawn and garden products with a strategy that stressed how the chemicals were actually responsible for "giving life," emphasizing the fertilizers and seeds over the herbicides and insecticides. Ortho also manufactures many specialty products for insect control, and there existed a small niche market for dealing with a tiny insect that has enormous destructive power: the fire ant. However, the "life-giving" strategy would be inappropriate for a product that was so deadly in dealing with the scourge of fire ants. Additionally, with a short infestation season in a limited geographic area in the southern and southeastern United States, Ortho did not want to devote a large budget to advertise its Antstop Orthene Fire Ant Killer, so it allocated only about $100,000 for marketing.

Working with his account team at BBDO West in Los Angeles, creative director David Lubars felt that radio, with its inexpensive production costs and quick response time, would be a better solution for Ortho's small budget than a slow-building local newspaper campaign. In 1996, Lubars turned to the one person on his staff who could create a high-impact in-your-face radio campaign to capture the violent antipathy people have for fire ants while at the same time using humor to soften the edge. Retained on staff was April Winchell, BBDO West's exclusive radio writer, who is married to BBDO senior art director Mick Kuisel. Together, they were partners in the radio production company they had formed in 1992, Radio Savant.

Lubars felt that only Winchell had the sensibility and talent to create the radio commercials for Antstop Fire Ant Killer. As the daughter of stage actor, voice-over, and grudgingly famous ventriloquist Paul Winchell, Winchell's "inherited brilliance and creative genes" brought her into contact at an early age with the magical world of performance and radio. By the age of 11, Winchell was already performing cartoon voice-overs. Later, she pursued her own career as a voice-over actress for animated films and starred as a musical comedienne and television sit-com writer. Winchell turned to advertising when Kuisel read some of her writing and suggested she would be good at copywriting because she *wasn't* trained in it and had not been burdened with the traditional rules of advertising.

Winchell is a truly theatrical person; her bawdy sense of humor, straight-shooting attitude, and unabashed love of telling it like it is made her the perfect candidate to write the Ortho ant killer spots. Despite naysayers at BBDO West who thought being a woman made her unqualified to write about bugs, Lubars and Winchell hit it off from the start of their professional relationship. He had faith in her ability and gave her carte blanche to handle the assignment, from scriptwriting to casting to production.

Winchell recalled that Lubars wasn't afraid to take the gloves off as a creative director and boss. Whenever she tried to do something self-conscious, he would immediately reject it. That's what happened with the first set of commercials Winchell scripted for the ant killer product. She attended the strategy briefing and then created a script in which a queen ant addressed her people in a speeded-up high voice that had, as Winchell put it, "a kind of a Dick Orkin-ish quality to it" (referring to Dick Orkin of the legendary writing team of Dick & Bert). Lubars knew it wasn't what he was looking for, and it certainly wasn't the kind of edgy, provocative writing that he knew he could get from Winchell.

However, he did allow Winchell to present the first scripts to Susan Boyle, the Ortho client. Much to her credit, Boyle rejected the first attempt by explaining to Winchell the emotional, almost visceral hatred that people in the South have for fire ants. She told Winchell about the havoc the ants wreak, swarming over pets, killing livestock and even, reportedly, a child. In fact, a 1997 article in the *Houston Chronicle* about the Antstop commercials quoted Senator Phil Gramm's estimate that fire ants were responsible for more than $300 million worth of damages annually in his home state of Texas. The moment of inspiration came for Winchell when she realized that the creative solution wasn't comical, it was a serious, emotional issue. When she understood that she didn't have to invent a reason for people to buy the product, because it responded to a real need with highly emotional drivers, Winchell had her hook. People didn't just want to simply get rid of the fire ants. They hated them, passionately, and they wanted them to die. And die mercilessly.

In total, Radio Savant created five commercials for Antstop Orthene Fire Ant Killer over a period of two years, Winchell crafting the spots and Kuisel filling in gags and "keeping her honest in her writing," according to Winchell. Mindful of the low budget for the campaign, Lubars knew that Winchell could produce the spots on a shoestring and develop a series of them quickly. No one, not Lubars, not Kuisel, not announcer Steve Morris who voiced the series of spots, not even Winchell herself suspected that the commercials would rip through the annual advertising awards competitions as powerfully as Antstop in a fire ant mound. What was just another day's work for Winchell paid off $100,000 as the grand prize in the Radio-Mercury Awards for the best commercial of 1997, with a coveted Gold Pencil from One Show, and in the $50,000 Grand Andy Award, the first time it was ever given for a radio commercial. Not only was the campaign a critical success according to a jury of its peers, the spots were also a huge commercial success—whenever they aired, the product charted a 30 to 35 percent increase in sales, according to John McDonald, business manager at Ortho.

The campaign itself is twistedly mischievous and painfully truthful. "When you're in the business of killing something," Winchell wrote for the One Show awards book, "it's almost in poor taste to talk about how well it works . . . so we threw political correctness out the window and found the lighter side of death." The spots capitalize on the simple truth of how people feel about fire ants: They hate them and want them dead. Winchell seized on those emotions and played on people's loathing. Kuisel, ever the adman, made sure the spots also described how the product should be applied, its ease of use, and other copy points.

Good humor shocks us into laughter when we expect one thing and we get its opposite. Winchell's spots for Antstop Fire Ant Killer put the truthful words of a vengeful, sarcastic fire ant hater into the voice of a serious, controlled announcer. Even as she was writing the spots, Winchell knew that she wanted the voice of announcer Steve Morris. Having worked with Morris for several years on other commercials, Winchell knew that he could do the classical 1950s announcer's voice of George Fennemen, straight man on Groucho Marx's television program, or the voice of Ted Baxter, news anchor character from the *Mary Tyler Moore* television show. Winchell recalled that Morris has the kind of voice that listeners are conditioned to believe, a voice that sounds true and wholesome, trustworthy and strong. Of course, those are the very qualities that Winchell's copy subverted to let Morris formally, yet with guarded glee, celebrate the killing power of Antstop Fire Ant Killer. The spots kindle in the listener the twisted pleasure of a naughty child burning bugs by focusing the sun's rays through a magnifying glass or using salt to dissolve snails and slugs—yet they are delivered in the mature voice of a grown-up. Therein lies the essential humor of the spot: the contradiction of a voice of authority condemning fire ants to "an excruciating, see-you-in-hell kind of death."

Every commercial in the series follows the cardinal rule of radio advertising and hooks the listener with the very first line. In "Instant Death," the copy begins, "Fire ants are not lovable. People do not want fire ant plush toys." The spot called "Sole Contribution" starts with the premise that "there's nothing good about fire ants. They don't pollinate your roses" or "make cute little sounds when they rub their legs together." In "Welts," Winchell contrasts the evil insects with honeybees and butterflies. When viewed as an entire campaign, the spots do have a format—a biting, satirical lead line, followed by a call for well-deserved death, and then a standardized explanation of the product's features and benefits. However, each commercial gives announcer Morris the opportunity to commiserate with the audience in their mutual hatred for the ants.

Radio history buffs will also recognize some of a classical announcer's rhetorical devices that Winchell crafted into the copy to capitalize on Morris's unctuous, beguilingly earnest delivery: starting sentences with the word *no*, as in "No, fire ants must die," or "No, my friend, . . ." or, breaking the professionalism of the third-person voice in "Sole Contribution," "And here's the really good part!" As Winchell described it, Morris's delivery has "all that old-time feel to it, but there's something subversive to it under the surface that's very disturbing."

As with many other successful campaigns—from Frebreg's Contadina spots to Golden's Laughing Cow cheese campaign to the Motel 6 ads—people in the media markets where the Antstop spots ran actually called radio stations and asked to hear the commercials at unscheduled times, beyond what the agency had purchased. One station reported being bothered by listeners calling for the ads over its music request line. But for advertisers, getting free airplay is a dream.

The spots do a great job of capturing people's attention. They also generated a buzz that added incredible value to the work. But one group of listeners didn't like what they heard. Members of People for the Ethical Treatment of Animals complained vehemently about the spots. "They didn't have a problem with our promoting a product that kills fire ants, but they deeply resented the fact that the presenter was simply too happy about it," commented Winchell in a special advertising supplement published by the Radio Advertising Bureau, sponsors of the Radio-Mercury Awards.

Some clients might get nervous when their commercials are criticized by a special interest group such as PETA, an organization so radical that its web site calls for Boy Scouts to "retire their fishing merit badges" for suffocating fish and for seafood lovers to stop eating lobsters. True, Ortho did at first respond to PETA's criticism by asking Radio Savant to reedit the spots to remove the tag line, "Kick fire ant butt!" and a few other incendiary lines. But Lubars and Winchell prevailed, contending that the product was *made* to kill, and the client restored the original lines. A year later, in 1997, during the next fire ant season, Radio Savant wrote two other commercials filled with sarcasm, one of them entitled "Apology." In it, announcer Morris offers a backhanded apology that allows him to say contritely, "I implied that killing fire ants was fun. For this I can only say, I'm sorry." He goes on to say how he will lobby for a fire ant postage stamp and provide them with better housing—and the copy still manages to work in the product's sales messages. It's the kind of apology that probably makes PETA sorry they ever requested it.

An article in *Adweek* magazine credited Winchell with "almost single-handedly reinventing radio as a red-hot genre." Anyone with that kind of buzz has a lot of bite to offer radio copywriters, including the following:

1. Be true to why you're selling the product.

"Everything is created in reaction to some need," Winchell says, "so talk about the need." Find out what the product's function is and work your concept around it. Don't give consumers reasons why they shouldn't be interested in your product. Ask yourself, does this commercial offer a reason to buy the product? Ridiculous concepts with stupid premises are sometimes cooked up for the sole purpose of setting up a dialogue or incorporating tuba music. To sell something as brilliantly and as simply as Radio Savant did for Ortho, just tell the truth. People *hate* fire ants. **Artfully, intelligently, and creatively find a way to express the truth of your product or service and you will be creating a commercial that helps sell it.**

2. Talk like people talk.

More than one radio writer would agree, from Joy Golden of the Laughing Cow cheese spots to Anne Winn and Garret Brown of Molson Golden fame, write your copy so

that people talk naturally. In normal conversation, people don't repeat what another person says, which is a contrivance of weak copywriters trying to repeat a copy point or product name. "Even if you don't listen to a lot of advertising, when you hear people talking unnaturally in a commercial, you'll know that there's something not to be trusted about it," says Winchell. Even if you're not writing natural-sounding dialogue—one of the hardest tasks in radio copywriting—honest copy grows out of how people really talk. Don't cram product features into every sentence. People speak in fragments, not full sentences. Run-on sentences are common, as are common everyday words. Listen to the announcer in Winchell's Antstop Fire Ant Killer commercials. Even the copy points sound realistic: "You don't want to *lug a big sack* of chemicals and a garden hose around the yard." That's how people really talk.

3. Consider the context.

Think about the station that will air your spot. It may be hard to know a complete media buy when you are just starting to work on the concept or the script, but knowing where and when your spots will run can help the creative process. You could be wedged between 15 soft hits, and every commercial playing in the cluster is going to have music behind it. Use music only if it's necessary to create a mood or make the point. Ironically, the Antstop Orthene Fire Ant Killer commercials were refused by a country music radio station because the commercials didn't have country music in them, but music wouldn't have been appropriate. **Many commercials fall prey to radio station formats—it's not uncommon for music used in a commercial to be arranged in the style of the station that will air it: country, rock-and-roll, classical, or hip-hop. In that case, it will just blend in with the audio "wallpaper."** Let your commercial speak for itself. What you want to say, and how you want to say it, is the first priority. Remember the clutter around the spot—if you want your commercial to stand out, you've got to know where it stands.

4. Keep your edges sharp.
Strangely enough, an advertising copywriter does everything possible to get people's attention, but then a client doesn't want to be noticed. Don't be afraid of controversy. "If you dumb it all the way down," says Winchell, "and sand all the points off of it, you'll have made a flat smooth thing." Give listeners a reason to listen to you and they'll pay attention. People hate fire ants. When Winchell learned how much people hate fire ants, she knew just how to sharpen her approach. It gave her the inspiration and the focus she needed to give her spots a real edge.

> ### Ortho Antstop Orthene Fire Ant Killer
> ### "Instant Death"
> Used by permission of Radio Savant

ANNCR: Fire ants are not lovable. People do not want fire ant plush toys. They aren't cuddly. They don't do little tricks. They just bite you and leave red, stinging welts that make you want to cry. That's why they have to die, and they have to die right now. You don't want them to have a long, lingering illness. You want death. A quick, excruciating, see-you-in-hell kind of death. You don't want to lug a bag of chemicals and a garden hose around the yard. It takes too long. And baits can take up to a week. No, my friend, what you want is Antstop Orthene Fire Ant Killer from Ortho. You put two teaspoons of Antstop around the mound and you're done. You don't even water it in. The scout ants bring it back into the mound. And this is the really good part: Everybody dies! Even the queen. It's that fast. And that's good. Because killing fire ants shouldn't be a full-time job. Even if it is pretty fun. Antstop Orthene Fire Ant Killer from Ortho. Kick fire ant butt. For best results, always follow label instructions.

Ortho Antstop Orthene Fire Ant Killer
"Sole Contribution"
Used by permission of Radio Savant

ANNCR: There's nothing good about fire ants. They don't pollinate your roses. They don't make cute little sounds when they rub their legs together. All they do is build a big mound in your yard and bite the hell out of anyone who gets near it. That's it. That's their sole contribution to mankind. And that's why they have to die. It's that simple. You cannot rehabilitate a fire ant. You have to kill him, his little red friends, and that big fat queen down there making more fire ants. Oh, you could lug a big sack of chemicals and a garden hose around the yard but that's about as fun as getting bit in the first place. No, what you need is Antstop Orthene Fire Ant Killer from Ortho. You put two teaspoons of Antstop around the mound and you're done. You don't even water it in. The scout ants track it back into the mound. And here's the really good part: Everybody dies! Even the queen. And while there's joy in all creatures living in harmony, it's nothing compared to wasting fire ants. Now, that's a rush. Antstop Orthene Fire Ant Killer from Ortho. Kick fire ant butt. For best results, always follow label instructions.

Ortho Antstop Orthene Fire Ant Killer
"Welts"
Used by permission of Radio Savant

ANNCR: Fire ants do not make honey. They don't have pretty wings. They don't bring you luck. They just bite you repeatedly, leaving painful, stinging welts. You cannot change a fire ant, no matter how much counseling you give him. Show me a man who stops to help a fire ant, and I'll show you a guy with welts on his butt. No, fire ants must die. And they must die quickly, before you've got so many mounds in your backyard you need a lunar module to get to the barbecue. You don't want baits, since those can take more than a week. And you don't want to lug a big sack of chemicals and a garden hose around the yard. No, what you need is Antstop Orthene Fire Ant Killer from Ortho. You put two teaspoons of Antstop around the mound and you're done. You don't even water it in. The scout ants come out, they track it back into the mound—and here's the really good part—everybody dies, including the queen. The queen is dead, vive la revolution! That's French, you know. Antstop Orthene Fire Ant Killer from Ortho. Kick fire ant butt. For best results, always follow label instructions.

⑪ Have You Heard the Latest? The Fundamentals of Radio's Future

Client: SmartShip.com
Production Company: World Wide
  Wadio
Date: 1999

Client: Twentieth Century
  Television/Fox
  The Simpson's Syndication
  Promo
Production Company: World Wide
  Wadio
Date: 1994

Client: B.Y.O.B.
Production Company: Outer
  Planet Radio
Date: 1997–1999

Client: Dairy Farmers of
  Washington
Agency: Evansgroup
Production Company: Outer
  Planet Radio
Date: 1995

Client: Southwest Airlines
Agency: GSD&M
Production Company: Oink Ink
Date: 1999

Client: King World/Jeopardy
Production Company: Oink Ink
Date: 2000

Client: Trico Wiper Blades
Agency: Gelia Wells & Mohr
Production Company: Sarley, Bigg
  & Bedder
Date: 1998–1999

Client: Jakada Blast Frozen Mocha
  Procter & Gamble
Production Company: Sarley, Bigg
  & Bedder
Date: 1999

Comedy is contextual. Comic radio commercials are no exception. Their humor is a unique product of their time, market geography, social mores, standards of acceptability, and hundreds of subconsciously understood references by the intended listeners. What might have evoked a loud chuckle in 1958—a joke about mooring a zeppelin or a spoof about Russians touring U.S. factories—falls flat 50 years later; the context is lost and the references are unclear.

However, despite differences in products, writing styles, performances, and cultural allusions, funny is still funny. When the joke is within its own context, when the elements of surprise, wordplay, or silliness are present, when the performance is delivered with comedic timing—that's what makes a radio commercial funny. Even with changes in what's acceptable on the airwaves (consider the sexual outrageousness of shock jocks Howard Stern and Opie and Anthony), today's humorous radio commercials reflect the attitudes of the late twentieth and early twenty-first centuries, as well as the modern influences that shaped the copywriters working their craft.

Rather than being influenced by the golden age of radio in the forties, today's radio creators cite influences as culturally varied and disparate as our contemporary society—from the zaniness of Warner Brothers cartoons broadcast on TV since the fifties to the edgier humor of Monty Python and the Firesign Theater in the late sixties to the gross-out humor of contemporary movies of the nineties such as *There's Something About Mary* and *American Pie*. Freed from some of the boundaries of FCC censorship, restrictive clients, and sometimes even taste, today's commercials are products of their time.

Yet there is still a legacy of craft and a homage to radio advertising history that is respected by almost every radio copywriter and producer working successfully today. Those featured in this chapter almost unanimously cite the Dick Orkin and Bert Berdis combination as an inspiration and influence. One writer/producer, while still in high school, used to disguise his voice and call Dick Orkin's company requesting a demo reel for "his agency." Another of today's radio writers still hoards his Dick and Bert demos recorded on Eva-Tone sound sheets, vinyl "record" pages that were inserted in advertising trade publications in the early seventies. And more than one contemporary writer tips his radio hat to Stan Freberg and Chuck Blore for their groundbreaking work.

Regardless of the writer, the product, or the shift in attitudes, there are still some fundamentals that make radio commercials funny in any era: namely, a well-written spot based on a simple, great idea performed by the best talent and produced to the highest standards. The commercials that win awards in today's competitions may be for products and services that were unimaginable 30 years ago—Internet companies that ship packages overnight, do-it-yourself microbreweries, or frozen coffee coolers—but their ability to make us laugh is timeless.

Humor in today's radio commercials is often an excellent barometer of the social changes over the past five years. During the dot-com boom and bust of the late 1990s, when start-up Internet companies were flush with millions in venture capital, they spent a lot of it on radio advertising with one sole purpose in mind: Drive an audience to the web site. SmartShip.com is an Internet company that was created as an information portal for consumers to find the best alternative for shipping packages. Mark Hawkins, one of the founders of SmartShip.com, knew that radio would be his only option to launch the company just prior to the Christmas rush, given a budget of only $100,000. "I'm a guerrilla marketer from way back," said Hawkins. "When I saw the kind of irreverence World Wide Wadio was offering, I knew that's what I wanted." Like many of the dot-com startups, the management of SmartShip.com sidestepped the usual advertising agency route and went directly to World Wide Wadio, one of the younger, hipper, and sillier radio production companies in Los Angeles.

Skipping the usual script approval process, or "read-it-over-the-phone" presentation, Hawkins trusted World Wide Wadio enough to let founder and head writer/producer Paul Fey and his sound engineer, Stewart Sloake, create and produce demos for a five-spot campaign that would introduce the new shipping service and drive listeners to SmartShip.com's package-shipping web site.

Of course, competing against big, established franchises like Mailboxes Etc. is a daunting task. But with a small media buy, airing only on Generation Y radio stations in the Greater Los Angeles area, SmartShip.com narrowed the odds in its favor. Targeting frantic shoppers in the days before Christmas to introduce its shipping service made the drive-time buy even more strategic. But the irreverently silly concept of the World Wide Wadio commercial drove over 100,000 hits to the web site after airing for only four days in 1999.

For the spot in the series titled, "Fifty Synonyms for Buttocks," Fey drew his inspiration for a commercial about last-minute gift shipping from real life. "Shipping holiday packages is a pain in the butt," Fey said. "Once I got that idea, the whole thing kind of wrote itself." The concept of the spot is simple: As the commonsensical voice of Steve Morris (the same actor who brought April Winchell's Ortho Fire Ant Killer spot to life) intones the numerous copy points, an electronically enhanced voice chimes in at strategically correct times to provide one of fifty synonyms for buttocks. To compile the list, which runs from *derriere* to *keister* and every butt in between, Fey collected scores of euphemisms from his coworkers, eventually developing a list long enough to "cover his ass in the studio." The contrast between Morris's grown-up announcer and the interjected silliness of naughty words for buttocks was strong enough to sweep five prestigious award categories at the Mobius Advertising Awards in Chicago in 2000, to win a trophy from the London International Advertising awards, and to receive kudos from the International Radio Festival of New York.

Another commercial for a syndicated animated television program shows just how far broadcast media has come since the decades when radio and television were fierce rivals for advertisers' dollars. Typical of the professional silliness that comes out of World Wide Wadio is a campaign created for 20th Century Television, Fox's distribution and production arm for the long-running animated hit, *The Simpsons,* when it went into syndication. Developed by Fey's writing partner, Walt Jaschek, the spot is simply a dramatic recitation of the after-school blackboard punishment writings of the animated character, Bart Simpson, read by the famous actor and singer, Robert Goulet. The blackboard writings are taken directly from the opening prologue to the animated show. "You can't come away remembering anything but the Simpsons," says Fey, "because the spot is all based on something that specifically comes out of the show that's funny to begin with." The spot reflects World Wide Wadio's attitude toward humorous radio. "It's one thing to write a clever little radio spot, fill in the blank, and you could put almost any product or service into it. The danger is you'll remember the funny and forget what it is you're selling."

The commercial combines the outrageous blackboard writings of Bart Simpson ("I will not trade pants with others"; "I will not do that thing with my tongue"; "A burp is not an answer") with the musically authoritative oration of Robert Goulet and the lilting cadences of a classical Strauss-style waltz. While he was on tour with *Camelot,* Goulet recorded the list of some 70 "Bartisms" taken from past scripts of *The Simpsons* via a digital phone patch. However, Goulet wasn't the first choice. Fey had wanted to use James Earl Jones, but he wasn't available. Goulet had once made an animated appearance on *The Simpsons,* playing to Bart and his friends in their tree house, and the singer was more than willing to be a part of the silliness again in the commercial. The spot won the Radio-Mercury Award for humor in 1994.

By the laws of physics and the realities of business marketing, radio has always been a regional medium. True, there have been national radio networks and, today, even satellite radio stations. But whether it's a local low-power college campus station or a 50,000-watt broadcaster covering half a state, radio programming and advertising has always sought to appeal to those audiences who were, as one announcer used to say, "within the sound of my voice." Radio advertising is an especially powerful and effective medium for small local businesses that want to reach customers in their immediate business market and for regional organizations whose message has appeal across geographically common but far-flung markets.

Two very twisted and very funny radio commercials from the Pacific Northwest demonstrate this type of regionalism. It's not surprising that these commercials come from the area that was the birthplace of Grunge Rock, Starbucks coffee, and innovative advertising from shops like Wieden and Kennedy and Borders, Perrin, Norrander in Portland, Oregon, and Wang Doody and Evansgroup (now Publicis) in Seattle, Washington. Perhaps it's something about being tucked away in a continental corner that has fostered its own insular brand of creativity.

A radio campaign for Be Your Own Brewmaster (B.Y.O.B.), a do-it-yourself microbrewery company in Fremont, Washington, was created by the broadcast boutique Outer Planet Radio in

Seattle. Three spots were produced in 1997 and aired only in Seattle over the next two years.

B.Y.O.B. provided the supplies, equipment, and facilities for hobbyists to brew, bottle, and label their own microbrews. While B.Y.O.B.'s owner had dabbled with radio, particularly local radio PR, he hadn't committed to a full ad campaign before working with Outer Planet's founder and creative director, Ken Bennett. Working very closely with sound designer Vince Werner of Seattle's Clatter & Din studios, Bennett created a series of three commercials for B.Y.O.B.

"I love taking an expected story and twisting it," says Bennett. His spots for B.Y.O.B. show his particular bent for slapstick humor. In the spot called "Classic Lines," which is a triumph of sound engineering by Werner, a do-it-yourself brewer named Dave has created his own beer commercials. He's done it, however, by "stealing" the music, setup lines, and style of big, established beer commercials. In seven different spoofs of radio and television beer commercials, Dave has amateurishly inserted the phrase "Dave's Beer" where the "real" brand name should appear. What makes this piece of advertising self-referential work is its verisimilitude. "I wanted to create the sound that you might hear if you were watching these as television spots with your eyes closed," said Werner. "The authenticity made the contrast so much more effective." Bennett worked closely with Werner to make sure the needle-drop music and "fake" voice-over announcers conjured up an image of the real thing. Its timeless "Dave"-versus-Goliath concept won a $20,000 prize for sound design in the Radio-Mercury Awards. In addition, sales at B.Y.O.B. immediately increased, as did call-ins to the radio stations that played it.

Another commercial from the Pacific Northwest that captures the region's offbeat humor was created by Bennett for the Dairy Farmers of Washington Association. At the time, he was a writer at the Evansgroup agency in Seattle, and the assignment was to get people to freeze butter—a highly profitable product for the associated dairy farmers—especially during the holidays. "It was such a strange assignment. I was laughing even before I started working on it," remembers Bennett. His final concept was appropriately simple for the Thanksgiving and Christmas holiday season: An overworked homemaker faced with holiday baking and cooking is visited by three magical elves who arrive to help her. But when Clippy, Snippy, and Lippy find that the "overworked human lady" hasn't frozen extra butter in her freezer, the elves become extremely irate. As one elf blurts out in his high-pitched elf voice, "What the hell were you thinking, anyway?" the spot spins an out-of-character twist on the traditional holiday elves that makes it even funnier.

The only thing funnier than the finished spot was the making of it. Bennett cast an ensemble of local Seattle comedic actors who worked quite well together. Forgoing the usual technique of pitch and speed processing the tape used by Ross Bagdasarian for his famous Alvin and the Chipmunks and the method used by Walt Kramer for his 1960s Fotomat campaign featuring out-of-character elves, sound designer Werner had the actors playing the elves actually inhale helium in the recording booth before their performance. The result made for some very funny, yet organic, voices as the helium sped up their vocal cords—and for a group of light-headed actors as well.

Not only have comedy styles changed with the times, clients have as well. Maverick Southwest Airlines has had one of the more successful ad campaigns in an industry cluttered with pretentious, self-serving, and misty-eyed commercials. The company's Austin, Texas, ad agency, GSD&M is a bit of a maverick itself, winning numerous awards for its intelligent work. As the long-standing agency for Southwest, GSD&M found a soul mate in the bicoastal radio production company, Oink Ink, located in New York and Los Angeles. Oink Ink's founder and creative director, Dan Price, along with his brother Jim, oversee the production work for the Southwest Airlines radio scripts that GSD&M send to them regularly. GSD&M creative director Mark Ray likes working with Oink Ink for its high-quality production and also because it's a good fit with the Southwest client. "At Southwest, they take their competition seriously, but not themselves," says Ray. The commercial called "Job Interview" demonstrates just what happens when intelligent GSD&M writing meets Oink Ink irreverence.

Produced in September 1999 and airing later that year, "Job Interview" is a sloppy "spit-com" interview between a prospective job candidate and her potential boss on the same day she has had a root canal operation. The spot is essentially a long setup for GSD&M's simple campaign line for Southwest, "Wanna get away?" According to Ray, who wrote the spot, "I wanted to create a comedic tension between the root canal and the job interview that would get answered by the tag line."

Both Ray and Price attribute much of the success of the spot to actress Jackie Hoffman, selected from some 80 actresses who auditioned for the part. "We kind of went overboard on casting," Price admitted, "but we wanted someone who could do the lisp and still be heard clearly." Countering Hoffman's slurpy performance is Randy Harris's bored executive interviewer, who adds an almost imperceptible "umm hmm" during her salavacious recitation of her qualifications. What makes the spot funny is not only the politically incorrect speech impediment, but the almost slapstick humor of combining a formal job interview with a disabling root canal. Who wouldn't want to get away?

Another commercial showcasing both Oink Ink's talent and a classic understanding of comedic timing is one written and produced for King World Productions, the company behind long-running game show, *Jeopardy*.

To promote the annual *Jeopardy* $100,000 Tournament of Champions, King World asked Oink Ink to have its stable of writers create a funny commercial that would bring some levity to the intellectual fisticuffs on the show. A commercial called "Trash Talkin'" was produced in December of 1999 and aired during the 2000 February TV ratings sweep.

In the 26-second spot, two brainy eggheads trade insults in a style commonly known in African-American culture as "playing a dozen." Actor Steve Ahern's nerd character slings it hard: "Your mama is so teratoid, she makes Rasputin appear to be as comely as Aphrodite!" "Oh, yeah," shoots back Bob Kaliban, "Well, *your* mama is as vapid as Mentha Spicata in a glass of Camellia sinesis!" The words are straight out of the dictionary, but it doesn't really matter whether the listener understands them. What's funny is the mental image of the pantywaist geniuses squaring off in their pretournament taunts. And, as with all great jokes, the humor is in the timing. Announcer Chris Murney simply adds after all the insults, "Let the trash talking begin."

Today's popular culture is often a complex mélange of movie and television references, celebrities, and silliness remixed and sampled, much like the creative conglomeration of some hip-hop music. Radio commercials have borrowed the technique as well. Although the style may sound like "now" in two commercials created by John Sarley, of the Los Angeles broadcast production firm of Sarley, Bigg & Bedder, the old-fashioned salesmanship sounds a lot like the traditional single-minded marketing of Rosser Reeves's unique selling proposition.

In a spot for Trico Exact Fit windshield wiper blades that Sarley wrote and produced in 1998 for the Gelia Wells & Mohr agency in upstate New York, the announcer imitates the eerily sardonic voice of *Twilight Zone*'s Rod Serling: "So . . . you're driving merrily along when suddenly . . ." the driver finds himself in a "Flash Storm" (the title of the spot) with worn-out wiper blades. What makes the commercial so effective is that Sarley combined the voices of two actors—Nancy Cartwright (the voice of Bart Simpson) and Frank Welker—with the sound effect of a squeaky wiper blade to give a voice to the inanimate wipers. According to Sarley, because "The natural rhythm of the wipers invites lyrics," the wipers repeat "You're so stupid, you're so stupid" (for not replacing the worn blades). After the announcer offers the simple sales message that Trico Exact Fit blades are "exact fit, easy to find, easy to install," the new wipers are singing a different tune: "You're smart, you're smart!" The spot was smart enough to win several Bests in the 1999 Mobius awards and to be included in the Chicago TV & Radio Hall of Fame. The commercial works as well as the Trico wiper blades because the humor is inherent in the product, and the digital effects are used only to enhance the sales message. The spot aired nationally from 1998 to 1999.

In a commercial produced in May 1999 for a new frozen coffee drink from Procter & Gamble and test-marketed in convenience stores in the Midwest, Sarley and his assistant, Mary Hill, again borrowed from popular culture. For the usually conservative P&G, Sarley promoted Jakada Blast Frozen Mocha with a reference to the teen horror film, *Scream*. In the commercial, an unseen and unknown stalker telephones a woman in his office: "Hello Paula. New sweater?" But rather than becoming sinister, the male caller begins to pitch Jakada Blast as a lift for the afternoon "slumps." The humor takes off on the word *slump*, as the two office mates get excitedly caught up in the product's "scrumptious frozen" taste. Here again, Sarley has paralleled a routine on television's *Saturday Night Live* in which comedian Rob Schneider played around with office mates' names and his own, calling himself the "copymeister." In the Jakada spot, the man and woman flirt shamelessly, as he calls her his "slumpty dumptress, slumperina, and finally, the one she likes best, "slump roast." Sarley supplied the man's voice, ad-libbing with actress Jane Lynch to create drama from the first five seconds of the spot. The commercial is zany, silly, and simple; however, the excited tone perfectly suits the product's caffeine benefits. "We were trying to sell the addiction," Sarley said, "not only the product."

All of these new commercials speak to the cultural sensibilities of today. But what is the future of humorous radio advertising? The answer to that question really has three parts. First, what is the future of radio itself? Second, what implications do future changes in radio have on broadcast advertising in general? And third, what will be funny tomorrow?

Currently, new technologies are coming to the world of radio broadcasting that offer the promise of unlimited channels, ultra-clear reception and global accessibility. Satellite radio, a concept that's been around for a decade, is now a reality, as two national broadcasters—XM Satellite Radio and Sirius Satellite Radio—have been granted FCC licenses. Several auto manufacturers have installed satellite radio receivers in some current-model cars, and portable satellite receivers are being marketed by consumer electronics companies. In an Internet article titled "How Satellite Radio Works" from Marshall Brain's How Stuff Works web site, writer Kevin Bonsor compares the impact of satellite service on radio to that of cable TV on network television 30 years ago. Satellite radio companies XM and Sirius are subscription-based services offering hundreds of channels of digital audio featuring music, talk, CNBC, NPR, and other programs. The technology of geosynchronous satellites and ground repeaters is too complex to cover here, but the important point is that the service is being positioned as "commercial-free." Subscribers will be able to get their digital music and talk, not only without static, but without commercial interruption. While that may spell danger to radio advertising, let's not forget the lessons of cable television. At its inception, one of the biggest selling points of cable television was the promise that it would be supported by paid subscribers, not through the sale of advertising time. However, as cable television evolved into ever-more-formatted channels—not unlike the growth of radio formats in the late fifties and early sixties—the potential to reach these demographically, psychographically delineated audiences was too enticing to ignore. A channel devoted to women, such as Lifetime, was especially attractive to advertisers of household products, feminine protection, over-the-counter drugs, and cosmetics. A 24-hour sports channel like ESPN

captured an audience of 25- to 54-year-old men so car companies, razors, and hair-growth products snapped up the available
advertising time. Satellite radio may start with the allure of
commercial-free programming, but the ability to reach a
national audience whose subscription information contributes
to a quantifiable demographic database may prove to be too
valuable and profitable for satellite stations and advertisers to
ignore. Jonathan Mitchell, a public radio producer who wrote
an essay for an Internet forum on "Perspectives on New
Media," believes that "as receivers for this emerging technology
become standard issue . . . more people will turn to satellite
radio" for national programming. Even with the initial prospect
of commercial-free satellite radio, the impact of a national
media network would harken back to the era of national radio
networks that existed in the 1930s and 1940s. For national
advertisers, this is an old opportunity made new again. The
impact on radio advertising, then, is that there will be more
opportunities for more commercials because there will be more
stations to run them.

Another emerging radio technology that is still in its infancy
is Internet radio. Currently, it's possible to log on to a number
of radio stations broadcasting over the Internet as dot-com ver-
sions of their AM/FM signals. This enables anyone anywhere
with a PC to listen to a station, regardless of distance. A jazz afi-
cionado in Tokyo can pick up a listener-supported jazz station
broadcasting from Newark, New Jersey. Sports stations in
England or Europe with the latest cricket and soccer scores can
be heard around the world via a computer or new stand-alone
Internet appliances.

The effect on radio advertising of this globalizing technology,
including the national satellite networks, is the same: Hundreds
of thousands more people will now hear an advertiser's commercial messages broadcast as part of the programming from
the originating station. The implications for creativity are enormous. Language barriers aside, for truly global brands like

Coke, Ford, Nike, and Kodak, Internet radio could be a huge opportunity to reach many people efficiently—as long as the creative message is culturally relevant. In the case of national brands, once satellite radio opens up to commercials, it's a chance to affordably reach a larger audience with a national radio buy. However, the creativity must play not only in Peoria, but also in Pittsburgh, Petaluma, Portland, and Poughkeepsie. Local stations will continue to broadcast local and regional commercials that are targeted to local consumers, much as before.

Finally, what will be funny 10 years from now? Because humor is contextual, it's difficult to predict what will make people laugh in 2012. But there are some constants. Says Ken Bennett of Outer Planet Radio, "Humor still has to fit into the context of what's current. While it may tap into funny family situations that are always universal and have been done many times, it becomes contemporary because writers are writing about it in ways that are happening at the moment." Even a long-standing gag about wives and husbands can hit home by adding the "twist of the moment," according to Bennett. Another creative radio producer, Dan Price of Oink Ink, feels that humorous radio is "just getting better and better." His assessment is based on his professional experience as a judge for many awards shows. Listening to commercials that win those awards gives some indication where funny radio is headed. One hears the cynicism and irreverence typical of contemporary life. Edgier concepts that break the traditional announcer-listener relationship are also prevalent in many commercials that acknowledge they are just commercials. Self-referential advertising that owns up to its job of selling is another currently popular style that may continue. Announcers and voice actors are becoming more natural and less affected, so they sound like real, quirky people instead of pompous shills.

Regardless of what tomorrow's humorous radio commercials may sound like, they will certainly draw on contemporary culture for their references. The winners will succeed as marketing communications and as comedic expressions because they will be grounded in the same lessons that have been around since radio advertising began, including the following:

1. Respect the fundamentals.
Even with all the advances in electronic editing, libraries of prerecorded music, and digital phone patches, current commercials are based on simple truths: a great script, great casting, and great performances. All the sound effects in the world won't save a poorly written commercial from falling flat. Bennett's helium-inspired elves would only be half as funny if the performances weren't sharp. The greatest actors in the world can't breathe life into a tongue-twisting mouthful of copy (e.g., Oink Ink's *Jeopardy* spot) if the context isn't appropriate. And casting the right actor can mean the difference between a light chuckle and something far more memorable. When Sarley first cast the announcer in the Trico wiper spot, he chose a booming-voice-type actor. When the sponsoring ad agency saw the Rod Serling voice characterization indicated in another spot, however, it made more sense for the script. Fey applied the same lesson in the World Wide Wadio spot for *The Simpsons*. "Originally, we thought of James Earl Jones as the contrast for Bart's silly lines." A little creative thinking by Fey's wife, Elaine Craig, who is a casting director, offered Goulet's musicality as a better choice. Keep the idea simple, keep the writing smart, choose the right people—three rules right for a winning radio commercial in any age.

2. Radio is a collaborative medium.
It may be true that radio is a showcase for the copywriter whose words are brought to life, but without the talents of the recording engineer and the actors, the script is nothing more than words on a page. All too often, a copywriter will bring a script directly to a recording session without first consulting with the

sound designer or engineer—the one person who has the talent, expertise, and experience to bring all the elements together into a cohesive commercial. **Involve your sound designer early on; ask for suggestion on music, sound effects, and recording techniques that can make your spot really unique.** Vince Werner, sound designer at Clatter & Din, was hugely responsible for making Bennett's scripts for B.Y.O.B. and Dairy Farmers of Washington into great commercials. Bennett worked with Werner to create the TV beer commercial effects, and it was Werner's idea to rent a tank of helium from a party supply store to speed up the actor's vocal cords. Fey was inspired by his casting director, who suggested Goulet as a celebrity voice for *The Simpsons* commercial. Most important of all, look to the actors as a valuable source of collaboration. A seasoned voice-over actor who has done thousands of commercials can bring an improvisational edge to even a well-honed script. Consider Randy Harris's "umm hmm" in the Southwest Airlines "Job Interview" spot, a line that wasn't in the script, or Jane Lynch's "slumpy" ad libs in Sarley, Bigg & Bedder's commercial for Jakada Blast. Price at Oink Ink even records his actors' auditions, occasionally catching a bit of creative lightning on tape. Once you have "a keeper in the can," let the actors have the comedic freedom to interpret a line here or there or to offer an alternative reading to a line.

3. Be here now.

Many of the commercials described here use contemporary references to shorthand a joke. The *Jeopardy* "Trash Talkin'" spot references the verbal taunts of prize fighters "playin' a dozen." The B.Y.O.B. spot "Classic Lines" parodies current beer commercials. The Trico Exact Fit wiper blade commercial "Flash Storm" features an imitation of television's scary auteur, Rod Serling. And the commercial for Jakada Blast alludes to the pop teen thriller film *Scream*. Even though these spots are firmly set in the "now," the timeless elements of parody, silliness, surprise are present. Topical humor can wear thin after the reference has passed and a joke or allusion that is understood by today's listeners might not play in years to come. **But by blending traditional comic techniques of great timing and expert performance with ideas and situations that click with today's funny sensibilities, you'll have a commercial that is not only in the "here and now" for 60 seconds, but one that may last forever.**

SmartShip.com
"Fifty Synonyms for Buttocks"
Used by permission of World Wide Wadio. All rights reserved. ©1999

ANNCR: Shipping holiday packages can be a major pain in the . . .

FAST, FUNNY VOICE: [*Overlaps tightly throughout*] butt/rear end/behind/buttocks.

ANNCR: It's true. Shipping holiday packages is *almost always* a pain in the . . .

FFV: tail/bottom/posterior/derriere.

ANNCR: In fact, it's usually *such* a pain in the . . .

FFV: cheeks/buns/caboose/heinie.

ANNCR: . . . that you *procrastinate.*

FFV: Kiester/fanny/can/tuchas.

ANNCR: Then, the only thing that's *more* of a pain in the . . .

FFV: rump roast.

ANNCR: . . . than holiday shopping . . . is *last-minute* holiday shopping.

FFV: tush/tushie/booty/bum.

ANNCR: Fortunately, there's SmartShip.com.

FFV: Gluteus maximus.

ANNCR: SmartShip.com helps you find the smartest, easiest, least-expensive way to ship, *especially* at the last minute.

FFV: Backside/backyard/back door/kazoo.

ANNCR: SmartShip.com gives you free information that lets you comparison-shop for the best rate . . .

FFV: moon.

ANNCR: . . . the best delivery guarantee . . .

FFV: sit-upon.

ANNCR: . . . and the most convenient drop-off schedule.

FFV: Po-po.

ANNCR: SmartShip.com even lets you print a map to the nearest drop-off location.

FFV: Patootie

ANNCR: Or tells you who can come *pick up* your package, saving *you* a major pain in the . . .

FFV: place where the sun don't shine.

ANNCR: Don't let holiday shipping be a pain in the . . .

FFV: arse/bucket/biscuits/mud flaps.

ANNCR: Use SmartShip.com. The way smart shipping is done.

FFV: Pooper.

Twentieth Television: The Simpsons
"Robert Goulet"

[*The female announcer is hushed and reverent. Mr. Goulet's performance is a highly dramatic reading that closely follows the meter of the classical melody underneath.*]

FEMALE ANNCR: And now, Mr. *Robert Goulet* reads from *The Writings of Bart* . . . the collected after-school *blackboard* writings of young *Bart Simpson.* Mr. Goulet . . .

MUSIC: [*Under*] [*Dignified, classical waltz*]

ROBERT GOULET: I will not trade pants with others.
I will not do that thing with my tongue.
I will not Xerox my butt.
A burp is not an answer.
I will not pledge allegiance to Bart.
I will not eat things for money.
I will not bring sheep to class.

I will not instigate revolution.
My name is not Doctor Death.

FEMALE ANNCR: To experience *all* of Bart's blackboard writings, watch *every classic episode* of *The Simpsons*.

ROBERT GOULET: I will not call the principal Spud Head.

FEMALE ANNCR: *The Simpsons.* Now five times a week.

MUSIC: [*Up, under, and out*]

> ### Dairy Farmers of Washington
> ### "Irate Elves"
> #### Used by permission of Outer Planet Radio

ANNCR: It was the night before the big holiday party, and Sally desperately needed help with last-minute preparations.

SALLY: I desperately need help with these last-minute preparations.

SFX: [*"magic" sound, as elves suddenly appear out of thin air*]

ELVES: Hi!!!

SALLY: What the—?

ELVES: We are three magic elves here to help you.

SALLY: Well, fine.

CLIPPY: I'm Clippy.

SNIPPY: I'm Snippy.

LIPPY: I'm Lippy.

CLIPPY: I'll finish these cookies.

SNIPPY: I'll make the gravy.

LIPPY: I'll bake this bread.

CLIPPY: Why don't you just go relax, overworked human lady.

SALLY: Well, great.

SNIPPY: Yes, just please tell us where you keep the butter.

SALLY: Butter? There should be some right here.

SFX: [*Butter dish*] Oh goodness, I guess I'm all out.

LIPPY: Of course, you have extra butter in the freezer.

SALLY: Well, no.

ALL: [*Very upset*]

CLIPPY: No butter in the freezer?

SNIPPY: Man!

LIPPY: This is extremely irritating for us.

CLIPPY: What the hell were you thinking, anyway?

SALLY: But—

SNIPPY: Without butter, we cannot sing and work merrily.

LIPPY: Without butter, this dinner will be as boring as your regular cooking.

SALLY: But you're elves. Can't you just get some butter out of thin air?

CLIPPY: That is not in our contract.

SNIPPY: Anyone with a clue would have frozen several pounds of butter.

LIPPY: To use through the holidays.

CLIPPY: We rode down the moonbeam for nothing.

LIPPY: I am so frustrated I am shaking.

SNIPPY: Show some elf control, Lippy.

B.Y.O.B.
"Classic Lines"
Used by permission of Outer Planet Radio

ANNCR 1: [*Classic, slick beer announcer*]
Enjoy the cool, clean taste of . . .

DAVE: [*Dubbed line, amateur-sounding production*]
Dave's Beer.

ANNCR 2: Tonight, let it be L—

DAVE: [*Dubbed in*] Dave's Beer.

ANNCR 3: For all you do, this—

DAVE: [*Dubbed in*] Dave's Beer.

ANNCR 3: is for you.

ANNCR 4: Bring out your best, bring out—

DAVE: [*Dubbed in*] Dave's Beer.

ANNCR 5: Brewed with pure Rocky Mountain . . .

DAVE: [*Dubbed in*] Fremont City.

ANNCR 5: . . . water

ANNCR 6: Next time, reach for an icy cold—

DAVE: [*Dubbed in*] Dave's Beer.

MAIN ANNCR: At B.Y.O.B. in Fremont, we'll help you
brew your own quality, microbrewed beer: pale ale,
wheat beer, amber ale, bitter, porter, stout. We'll
provide all the supplies and instruction and even help
you design your own cool-looking color label. How you
tell people about your beer, after it's done, is up to you.

ANNCR 2: Weekends were made for . . .

DAVE: [*Dubbed in*] Dave's Beer.

MAIN ANNCR: Call B.Y.O.B.—that's Be Your Own Brewmaster—at 634-BREW.

B.Y.O.B.
"Bunch of Lies"
Used by permission of Outer Planet Radio

WOMAN: [*Bad overacting*] You mean it was all a bunch of lies!!?

MAN: Listen Gloria—I can explain.

WOMAN: You *don't* own a multinational shipping company?

MAN: Umm, no.

WOMAN: You're not a software millionaire?

MAN: No.

WOMAN: You haven't played in the World Series three times?

MAN: 'Fraid not.

WOMAN: How could I have been such a fool?!?! You never walked on the moon?

MAN: No.

WOMAN: You didn't invent rap?

MAN: Sorry.

WOMAN: You don't rescue flood victims in obscure Third World countries in your spare time?

MAN: No.

WOMAN: You didn't serve with General MacArthur?

MAN: No.

WOMAN: I was so blind?!?! You're not really a brewmaster with your own custom-labeled microbrewed beers?

MAN: Wait! That part was true! See?

WOMAN: Dave's Beer. Your name and picture are on the label—you told the truth!

MAN: Do you still love me, Gloria?

WOMAN: Oh, yes!

ANNCR: At B.Y.O.B. in Fremont, you can brew your own quality, microbrewed beer: pale ale, wheat beer, amber ale, bitter, porter, stout. We'll provide all the supplies and know-how and even help you design your own cool-looking color label. Make your own microwbrewed beer at B.Y.O.B. in Fremont . . . a worthy achievement.

WOMAN: You didn't build the Taj Mahal?

MAN: No, Gloria—but I did make this beer.

> ### King World Jeopardy Tournament of Champions
> ### "Trash Talkin'"
> Used by Permission of Oink Ink

GUY 1: Your mama is so teratoid, she makes Rasputin appear to be as comely as Aphrodite!

GUY 2: Oh, yeah?

GUY: 1: Yeah!

GUY 2: Well, *your* mama is as vapid as Mentha Spicata in a glass of Camellia sinensis!

GUY 1: Well, I think I saw your brother.

GUY 2: What?!

GUY 1: He was in a streptobacilius culture.

GUY 2: Ah, you wouldn't know a streptobacilius from a streptomyeces.

GUY 1: Oh, yeah!

GUY 1 & 2: [*Arguing/under*]

ANNC: The *Jeopardy* $100,000 Tournament of Champions is coming.

GUY 1: Narcissist!

GUY 2: Sycophant!

ANNC: Let the trash talking begin.

MUSIC OUT: [*Jeopardy theme*]

> ### Southwest Airlines
> ### "Job Interview"
> #### Used by permission of GSD&M

SFX: [*Phone ringing/office ambience*]

SCHMIDT: So, Ms. Harris, what makes you think you are
a good fit with us here at Schmidt, Starks, and
Supranski?

HARRIS: Oh, thir. There'th tho many reathons. I
thpecialized in rethearch and theoretical thtudies for
theveal yearth at the Thouthampton Inthtitute,

SCHMIDT: Umm hmm.

HARRIS: . . . pretheded by intentihive graduate thtudies
at Thracuthe. Thertainly, my thkills are well thuited for
a posithion here at Thmidt, Thtarks, and
Thump . . . thump . . .

SCHMIDT: Supranski?

HARRIS: Thankth . . .

ANNC 1: A job interview . . . and a root canal. On the
same day. Wanna get away?

SFX: [*Ding of airplane PA system*]

ANNC 1: Get the heck out of there with Southwest Airlines. Fly coast-to-coast for $99 or less each way with seven-day advance round-trip purchase. Fly now through March 31st. Purchase tickets by November 3rd.

HARRIS: It was nithe meeting you, thir.

SCHMIDT: Yes, we'll get back to you thoon. *Soon.*

ANNCR 1: Southwest Airlines. A symbol of freedom. Call 1-800-FLY SWA. [*Script used for demonstration purposes only. Offer and fare not valid as a promotion.*]

Procter & Gamble, Jakada Blast
"Slumpy"
Used by permission of Sarley, Bigg & Bedder

SFX: [*Office ambience, phone ring, pickup*]

WOMAN: [*Yawn*] Hello?

MAN: (*Deep and mysterious*) Hello, Paula. New sweater?

WOMAN: Who is this?

MAN: You're slumping at your desk again.

WOMAN: I am?

MAN: Looks like you could use a lift, Slumpy!

WOMAN: Wha . . . what did you have in mind?

MAN: You need a Jakada Blast! Fast!

WOMAN: A Jakada *what?*

MAN: Doh, Slump-a-lina! You've never heard of a Jakada Blast?

WOMAN: Well, actually, I . . .

MAN: It's a scrumptious frozen mocha that cools you deep down and picks ya right up!

WOMAN: Should I write this down?

MAN: No! Now bag those pie charts and bee-line your behind down to the nearest Jakada Blast Frozen Blending Machine. . . .

WOMAN: Okay . . .

MAN: Then shout, "I gotta getta Jakada Blast!"

WOMAN: (*Shouting*) I gotta getta Jak . . . !!!

MAN: No, not now!

WOMAN: Oh. I'm sorry!

MAN: So you'll go?

WOMAN: I'll go.

MAN: Good.

WOMAN: Right now.

MAN: Giddyup, my slumpty dumptress!

WOMAN: Your what?

MAN: Sl . . . forget that one! How 'bout Slumperina?

WOMAN: Who?

MAN: Slumpity Do-dah!

WOMAN: Uhmm . . .

MAN: Slumproast! [*Under/out*]

WOMAN: I like that.

ANNCR: Hey! Wanna dump the slumps? You gotta getta Jakada! New Jakada Blast Frozen Mocha!

> ### Gelia Wells & Mohr, Trico Exact Fit Wiper Blades
> ### "Flash Storm"
> #### Used by permission of Sarley, Bigg & Bedder

ANNC: So . . . you're driving merrily along when suddenly . . .

SFX: [*Thunderclap followed by rain*]

ANNC: A flash storm. No problem. You turn on your wipers and . . .

SFX: [*Bad windshield wipers, rhythmic scraping sound*]

ANNC: Big problem. Your windshield becomes a hellish blur of bugs, grit, and mud. Your worn-out wipers wheeze and chug flaccidly back and forth as if to say . . .

SFX: [*Processed squeaky voices in wiper rhythm*] "You're so stupid. You're so stupid. You're so stupid!"

ANNC: . . . Echoing every negative thought you've ever had about yourself, because you tried changing your blades once but got so flustered you blubbered like a big baby. You poor boob. Haven't you heard about Exact Fit wiper blades? Exact Fit blades are easy to install. No confusing parts to assemble. No threat to your self-esteem. Just click them on and go. After all, wouldn't you rather hear your wipers say . . .

SFX: [*Rain*]

SFX: [*Processed pleasant wiper voices in wiper rhythm*] "You're smart, you're smart, you're smart!"

ANNC: You bet you would. Exact Fit wiper blades from Trico. Easy to find, easier to install.

Bibliography

REFERENCES

Benny, Mary Livingstone, *Jack Benny: A Biography,* Doubleday & Co., 1978.

Dobson, Lawrence, *When Advertising Tried Harder: The Sixties: The Golden Age of American Advertising,* Friendly Press, 1984.

Douglas, Susan J., *Listening In: Radio and the American Imagination,* Times Books, 1999.

Freberg, Stan, *It Only Hurts When I Laugh,* Times Books, 1988.

Gossage, Howard Luck, *The Book of Gossage: A Compilation,* Rotzoll, Graham, Munsey (eds.), The Copy Workshop, 1986.

Josefsberg, Milt, *The Jack Benny Show: The Life and Times of America's Best Loved Entertainer,* Arlington House, 1977.

Maltin, Leonard, *The Great American Broadcast,* Dutton, 1997.

Nachman, Gerald, *Raised on Radio,* Pantheon, 1998.

Schulberg, Bob, *Radio Advertising: The Authoritative Handbook,* NTC Business Books, 1994.

Sivulka, Julliann, *Soap, Sex and Cigarettes: A Cultural History of American Advertising,* Wadsworth Publishing Company, 1998.

Stiller, Jerry, *Married to Laughter: A Love Story Featuring Anne Meara,* Simon & Schuster, 2000.

Contacts

Bert Berdis & Company
1956 Cahuenga Blvd.
Hollywood, CA 90028
323-464-7261
www.bertberdisandco.com

Bob & Ray
To order Bob & Ray cassettes, or for a catalog, visit
www.bobandray.com, or call 1-800-528-4424.

Stan Freberg
Freberg Ltd.
310-474-2184

Joy Radio, Inc.
60 West 57th St.
New York, NY 10019
212-957-1058

Mal Sharpe
Man-on-the-Street Productions, Inc.
2515 Russell St.
Berkeley, CA 94705
510-843-7655
mal@sharpeworld.com

Oink Ink
265 Madison Ave. #300
New York, NY 10016
1119 Colorado Ave., Suite 5
Santa Monica, CA 90401
800-776-OINK
www.oinkradio.com

Dick Orkin's Radio Ranch
1140 N. La Brea Ave.
Los Angeles, CA 90038
213-462-4966
doranch@aol.com
www.radio-ranch.com

Outer Planet Radio
1501 Western Ave., Suite 302
Seattle, WA 98101
206-624-9700
www.outerplanetradio.com

Radio Savant
info@radiosavant.com

The Radio Spot
Thomas Hripko
2311 Abrams Rd., Suite 100
Dallas, TX 75214
214-824-5575
www.theradiospot.com

The Richards Group
8750 N. Central Expwy., Suite 1200
Dallas, Texas 75231-6437
214-891-5700
www.therichardsgroup.com

Sarley, Bigg & Bedder
1644 North Stanley Ave.
Hollywood, CA 90046
sarleybigg@aol.com

2voices.com
Anne Winn & Garrett Brown
winnanne@hotmail.com
garrettcam@aol.com

World Wide Wadio
6464 Sunset Blvd., 11th floor
Hollywood, CA 90028
323-957-3399
www.wadio.com

CD Tracks and Credits

1. Piels beer, "Brand X" Used by permission ©℗ 1967, 1968, 1990, The Radio Foundation, Inc. All rights reserved.
2. Piels beer, "Russian Brewer," ©℗ 1967, 1968, 1990, The Radio Foundation, Inc. All rights reserved.
3. Contadina Tomato Paste, "Empire State Building/Who Puts Eight Great Tomatoes in That Little Bitty Can?" Used by permission, Freberg, Ltd.
4. Bell Brand Potato Chips, "Shoe Polish" Used by permission, Man-on-the-Street Productions, 2001.
5. Bell Brand Potato Chips, "Pickle," Used by permission Man-on-the-Street Productions, 2001.
6. *Time* Magazine, "Banana Boat" Used by permission, Dick Orkin & Bert Berdis.
7. *Time* Magazine, "Puffy Sleeves" Used by permission, Dick Orkin & Bert Berdis.
8. *Time* Magazine, "Fuchi Manuli" Used by permission, Dick Orkin & Bert Berdis.
9. Laughing Cow cheese, "Valley Girl I" Used by permission, Joy Radio, Inc.
10. Laughing Cow cheese, "Craving" Used by permission, Joy Radio, Inc.

11. Laughing Cow cheese, "Hot Tub Brunch" Used by permission, Joy Radio, Inc.

12. Molson Beer, "Border Crossing" Used by permission, Two-Voices, Inc.

13. Molson Beer, "Designated Driver" Used by permission, TwoVoices, Inc.

14. Molson Beer, "Comedy Club" Used by permission, Two-Voices, Inc.

15. Motel 6, "Comparison," Used by permission, Accor Economy Lodging.

16. Motel 6, "Deficit Reduction" Used by permission, Accor Economy Lodging.

17. Ortho Antstop Fire Ant Killer, "Sole Contribution" Used by permission, Radio Savant.

18. Ortho Antstop Fire Ant Killer, "Instant Death" Used by permission, Radio Savant.

19. SmartShip.com, "Fifty Synonyms for Buttocks" Used by permission, World Wide Wadio.

20. Twentieth Television, The Simpsons, "Robert Goulet" Used by permission, World Wide Wadio.

21. Dairy Farmers of Washington, "Irate Elves" Used by permission, Outer Planet Radio.

22. B.Y.O.B., "Classic Lines" Used by permission, Outer Planet Radio.

23. King World, Jeopardy "Trash Talkin" Used by permission, Oink Ink Radio.

24. Jakada Blast, "Slumpy" Used by permission, Sarley, Bigg & Bedder.

25. Trico Exact Fit Wiper Blades, "Flash Storm" Used by permission, Sarley, Bigg & Bedder.

Index

A

Absolut vodka, 99
Accor, 139
Advertising. *See* Commercials
Ahern, Steve, 177
Alch, Alan, x
Alka-Seltzer, 65
Allen, Fred, 3–4, 7
Allen, Steve, 44
American Tobacco, 2, 6
Anacin, 14
Anderson, Ernie, 46
Anheuser-Busch, xxi
Antique Boutique, The, xi
Atkinson, Brooks, 14
Austin, Phil, x
Avis Rent A Car, 65

B

Bales, Mike, 142
Balliett, Whitney, 11
Barzman, Alan, xi
BBDO West, Ortho campaign
    by, 156–161
Beany & Cecil, 46
Bell Brand potato chips,
    41–59

"Chanting" commercial, 49,
    57–58
"Chips on Floor" commercial,
    47, 56
history of, 45–46
"Pickle" commercial, 47,
    52–53
"Shoe Polish" commercial, 48,
    54–55
"Test of Fire" commercial,
    47–48, 58–59
TV commercials for, 46
Bennett, Ken, 174–175, 181
Benny, Jack, 4–7, 13
Berdis, Bert, xi, xvi, 75–85
Bergman, Peter, x
Bert Berdis & Company, xxi,
    83
Be Your Own Brewmaster
    (B.Y.O.B.), campaign for,
    173–174
awards won by, 174
"Bunch of Lies" commercial,
    191–192
"Classic Lines" commercial,
    174, 189–191
Blore, Chuck, xxi, 45

Blue Nun wine, 61–72
  awards won by campaign, 69
  feminist commercial, 67–68
  history of, 66
  manicotti commercial, 67
  singles resort commercial, 66
Bob and Ray, xxi, xxiii, 11–25
Bodett, Tom, xvi, xxiii, 137–147
Bonsor, Kevin, 179
Boyle, Susan, 157
Brass Rail, the, 118
Brinkley, Alan, 76
Brisacker-Wheeler, Contadina
    campaign by, 29–40
Broun, Heywood, 6
Brown, Garrett, xxi, 117–128
Budweiser, xxi
Burns, Jack, 64

C
Cadbury Callard & Bowser,
    xiv–xv
California Avocado Growers, ix
Calnan, Jack, 45
Canada Dry, 4, 5
Cartwright, Nancy, 177
Caterpillar, xii
Cavett, Dick, 77
Cellular One, 50
Chevrolet, 5
Chicken Man, 82
Child, Julia, 63
Cleese, John, xiv–xv
Cliff Freeman & Partners, xxi
Cohen, Julie, 105
Commercials:
  brand comparisons in, 46
  hard-sell vs. soft-sell, 13–14
  on radio (see Radio commer-
    cials)
  radio versus TV, xx, 16
  writing of, 79
Contadina Foods, xvi, xxii–xxiii,
    27–40

Empire State Building com-
    mercial, 33–34, 38–40
  history of, 32
Continental Airlines, x–xi
Costello, Richard, 99, 101
Coyle, Jim, 43–46
Coyne, Jim, 79
Crusader Rabbit, 46

D
Dairy Farmers of Washington
    Association, "Irate Elves"
    commercial, 174–175,
    187–189
Dale, Arden, 2
Dancer Fitzgerald Sample, Mol-
    son campaign of, 120–121
Dash, 14
Davidson, Ralph, 82
DDB Chicago, xxi
Deering, Milo, 141
Della Femina, Jerry, 64–66, 68
Della Femina, Travisano & Part-
    ners, campaign for Blue
    Nun, 63–72
Diamond, Selma, 102
Dick and Bert, xv, xxi, 75–85,
    170
Doyle Dane Bernbach,
    64–65
Drysdale, Don, x
Durkee, Norm, xi

E
Einbinder Flypaper, 12
Elliott, Bob, xxi, xxii, 11–22
Enberg, Dick, x

F
Fallon, xxi
Fashion Institute of Technology,
    xii
Faulkner, Tom, 141
Fey, Paul, 171–173

The Fibber McGee and Molly Show, 4
Finch, Dee, 12
Firesign Theater, x
Flynn, Miriam, 80
Fotomat, xiv
Fowler, David, 2, 139–143
Freberg, Donovan, xxii
Freberg, Stan, xi, xx, xxi
  awards won by, 29
  campaign for Contadina, 29–40
Fromageries Bel (FroBel), 100

G
General Foods, 3
General Motors, 3
General Tire, 5
Gerald McBoingBoing, 15
Godfrey, Arthur, 7
Golden, Joy, xvi, xxi, 99–108
Goodby, Silverstein & Partners, xxi
Gossage, Howard, 29, 31–32, 34
Goulding, Ray, xxi, 11–22
Goulding-Elliott-Graham Productions, 16
Goulet, Robert, 172–173
Graham, Ed Jr., 13–16, 20
Granny Goose Foods, 45
Grape-Nuts, 5
GSD&M, Southwest Airlines campaign by, 175–176

H
Harris, Randy, 176
Hawkins, Mark, 171
Hewlett-Packard, xxi
Hill, George Washington, 6
Hill, Mary, 178
Hoffman, Jackie, 176
Hollander, Jason, 76
Hollywood Video, xxi
Honeybaked Hams®, xii

Honig-Cooper & Harrington, Bell Brand campaign by, 45–59
Hopkins, Claude, 3
Hripko, Thomas, 140, 142, 145
Hunt's, 32, 35

I
Internet radio, 180–181

J
Jakada Blast Frozen Mocha, "Slumpy" commercial, 178, 195–197
Jaschek, Walt, 172
Jell-O, 5, 6
Jeopardy, 176–177
  "Trash Talkin'" commercial, 176–177, 193–194
JIF, 14
Josefsberg, Milt, 4, 6

K
Kaiser Aluminum, 36
Kaliban, Bob, 177
Kavanagh, J. Penn, 69
KCSB-FM, x
Kelly, Christina, 122
Kent cigarettes, 30
Klein, Bob, xi, 117
Kodak radio network, 118
KPFK, x
Kramer, Walt, xiv
Kretchford Braid and Tassel, 12
Kuisel, Mick, 155, 156, 158

L
Laughing Cow, xvi, 97–113
  "Craving" commercial, 102–103, 109–110
  "Enid and Galaxy" commercial, 112–113
  history of, 100

Laughing Cow (*Continued*)
   "Hot Tub Brunch" commer-
      cial, 103, 110
   "Valley Girl" commercials,
      104–105, 108–109,
      111
Lee Apparel, xxi
Leeds, Peter, 33
*Let's Run It Up the Flagpole and
   See Who Salutes,* ix–x
Letterman, Dave, 44
Lindner, Bob, 143
Lintas, Molson campaign by,
   121–122
Lipton, Lynn, 102
Little Caesar, xxi
Livingstone, Mary (Mrs. Jack
   Benny), 6
Longfield, David, 142
Lubars, David, 156
Luce, Henry, 76
Lux Soap, 3
Lynch, Jane, 178

M
Maltin, Leonard, 4
Marrici, Marty, 34–35
May, Elaine, 64, 119
McCarthy, Joe, 138
McDonald, John, 158
Meara, Anne, xxi, 63–71
Michigan Bell, 118
Mitchell, Jonathan, 180
Molson, 115–134
   "Border Crossing" commer-
      cial, 119, 120, 124–125,
      128–130
   "Comedy Club" commercial,
      125–126, 132–134
   "Designated Driver" commer-
      cial, 123, 125, 130–132
Morgan, Harry, 7
Morris, Steve, 158, 159,
   171

Motel 6, xvi, xxiii, 135–151
   "Aunt Josephine" commercial,
      150
   awards won by commercials,
      145–146
   "Comparison #2" commer-
      cial, 142, 144, 148
   "Deficit Reduction" com-
      mercial, 144–145,
      148–149
   "Financial Guru" commercial,
      151
   history of, 138
   "Singing Phone Number"
      commercial, 145
   "Strike 3" commercial,
      149–150
Mr. Magoo, 15
Murney, Chris, 177

N
New England Doll and Novelty,
   12
Nichols, Mike, 64, 119
Novak, Gene, 118

O
Oakner, Larry:
   career of, x–xii
   commercials created by,
      xii
Oakner, Mervyn, ix
Ogilvy, David, 3
Oink Ink, xx, 175–176
On the Road, 31
O'Reilly, Cathy, 69
Orkin, Dick, xi, xxi,
   75–85
Ortho Fire Ant Killer, xiii,
   xvi, 153–165
   awards won by commercials,
      158
   "Instant Death" commercial,
      159, 163–164

"Sole Contribution" commercial, 159, 164
"Welts" commercial, 159, 165
Outer Planet Radio, 173–174

P

Pacific Power and Light, xi, 50
Papert Koenig, 20
People for the Ethical Treatment of Animals (PETA), 160–161
People magazine, 77
Pepsodent, 14
Piel, Bert and Harry, 14–15
Piel Brothers beer, xxiii, 9–25
  brand comparison commercial, 17, 22–24
  history of, 13
  remote broadcast commercial, 16, 18
  Russian translator commercial, 17–18, 24–25
  TV commercials for, 15
Ponctillos pizza, 50
Presby, Tania, xi
Price, Dan, xx, 175, 181
Price, Jim, 175
Provident National Bank, 118

R

Radio:
  future of, 178–182
  loss of audience to TV, 12–13
  timeliness of, 117
Radio Advertising Bureau, xix
Radio commercials:
  composing music for, 141–142, 162
  editing of, 124
  historical context of, xiii, xxii–xxiii, 30–31, 43–44, 119–120, 122, 169
  history of, 2–7, 30
  lessons from, 20–22, 35–38, 50–52, 70–72, 83–85, 106–108, 126–128, 146–147, 161–163, 182–184
  planning of, 48–49
  on satellite/Internet radio, 179–181
  use of humor in, xix–xxiii, 1–2, 69, 81–82
  use of sound effects in, 68, 84, 124, 127–128
  voice casting for, 65, 102, 105–106, 119, 140–141, 159, 173, 182, 183
Radio-Mercury awards, xix
Radio Ranch, 83
Radio Savant, xxii, xxiii
  Ortho campaign by, 155–165
Ray, Mark, 176
Rayburn, Gene, 12
Reaske, Peter, 121–122
Reeves, Rosser, 3, 13–14
Reilly, Charles Nelson, 77
Renfro, Mike, 142
Richards, Stan, 142
The Richards Group, Motel 6 campaign by, 137–151
Rumrill-Hoyt, Molson campaign by, 118–120
Ryerson, Annie, 80

S

Sarley, John, 177–178
Satellite radio, 179–180
Schneiders, Frank, 101
Schreiber, Avery, 64
Shannon, Ray, 120
Sharpe, Mal, xi, xv, xvi, xxi, 140
  campaign for Bell Brand, 43–52
Sidebotham, Jack, 15
Simon, Scott, 45

The Simpsons, "Robert Goulet"
    commercial, 172–173,
    186–187
  awards won by, 173
Sivulka, Julliann, 31
Skenazy, Lenore, 18–19
Sloake, Stewart, 171
SmartShip.com, 170–171
  awards won by commercial,
    172
  "Fifty Synonyms for But-
    tocks" commercial,
    171–172, 184–186
Smith, Jerry, 77
Smothers, Dick and Tom, 140
Southern California Rambler
    Dealers, ix
Southwest Airlines, 175–176
  "Job Interview" commercial,
    176, 194–195
Sponsors:
  power over commercials' con-
    tent, 3
  spoofing of by radio comedi-
    ans, 3–6
STEADICAM®, 121
Stewart, Carl, 99
Stiles, Lynn, xv
Stiller, Jerry, xxi, 63–71
Stroh Brewery, 20
Studer, Eric, 143

T

TBWA, Laughing Cow cam-
    paign by, 99–113
Texaco, 4
Thrasher, Hugh, 138, 140
Thriftimart, ix
Time magazine, xv, 73–96
  "Banana Boat" commercial,
    78, 80, 85–87
  "Fuchi Manuli" commercial,
    81, 90–91
  history of, 75, 76

"Puffy Sleeves" commercial,
    78, 80, 88–89
"Ripper" commercial, 78,
    94–96
"Train Station" commercial,
    81, 92–94
Tragos, Bill, 99, 101
Trico, 177–178
  awards won for commercials,
    178
  "Flash Storm" commercial,
    177–178, 197–198

U

Underhill, Rod, 138

V

Volkswagen, 65

W

Welker, Frank, 177
Werman & Schorr, Molson cam-
    paign by, 118
WHDH, 11
Whippet Motor Car Company,
    12
Wilson, Don, 6
Winchell, April, xvi, xxi, xxii,
    155–160
  awards won by, 158
Winn, Anne, xxi, 117–127
WINS, 12, 13
World Wide Wadio, 171–173
Wynn, Ed, 4
Wyse Agency, 20

Y

Young & Rubicam, 6
  Molson campaign by, 122
  Piels beer campaign by, 9–25
  Time campaign by, 75–96

Z

Zappa, Moonunit, 104

About the CD-ROM

INTRODUCTION

The files on the enclosed CD-ROM were created using audio software for PCs. In order to use the files you will need to have software capable of reading an audio CD-ROM.

SYSTEM REQUIREMENTS

- IBM PC or compatible computer
- CD-ROM drive
- Windows 95 or later
- Audio software (e.g., Windows Media Player, Real Audio)

USING THE FILES

Loading Files

To use the audio files launch Windows Explorer. Select the appropriate CD-ROM drive on the left-hand side. A list of files should appear on the right-hand side. Double click on the file you want to use.

USER ASSISTANCE

If you need assistance with the files or if you have a damaged CD-ROM, please contact Wiley Technical Support at:

Phone: (212) 850-6753
Fax: (212) 850-6800 (Attention: Wiley Technical Support)
E-mail: *techhelp@wiley.com*
URL: *www.wiley.com/techsupport*

To place additional orders or to request information about other Wiley products, please call (800) 225-5945.

About the Author

LARRY OAKNER has been creating, producing, and teaching advertising for almost three decades. As a copywriter and creative director for advertising agencies on the West and East Coasts, he has written, produced, and directed hundreds of radio commercials, many winning prominent regional and national awards, including Finalist in the prestigious Radio-Mercury Awards sponsored by the Radio Advertising Bureau. In the course of his career in advertising, he has worked with many of the people featured in *And Now a Few Laughs From Our Sponsor.* Oakner also serves as adjunct professor at State University of New York's Fashion Institute of Technology where he teaches radio and television copywriting. He lives in New York.

For information about the CD-ROM see the **About the CD-ROM** section on pages 213–214.

CUSTOMER NOTE: IF THIS BOOK IS ACCOMPANIED BY SOFTWARE, PLEASE READ THE FOLLOWING BEFORE OPENING THE PACKAGE.

This software contains files to help you utilize the models described in the accompanying book. By opening the package, you are agreeing to be bound by the following agreement:

This software product is protected by copyright and all rights are reserved by the author, John Wiley & Sons, Inc., or their licensors. You are licensed to use this software on a single computer. Copying the software to another medium or format for use on a single computer does not violate the U.S. Copyright Law. Copying the software for any other purpose is a violation of the U.S. Copyright Law.

This software product is sold as is without warranty of any kind, either express or implied, including but not limited to the implied warranty of merchantability and fitness for a particular purpose. Neither Wiley nor its dealers or distributors assumes any liability for any alleged or actual damages arising from the use of or the inability to use this software. (Some states do not allow the exclusion of implied warranties, so the exclusion may not apply to you.)